DISCIPLE *for* LIFE

Letters of the Revelation

To the One Who Conquers

D. A. Horton

with *Brandon D. Smith*

LifeWay Press® • Nashville, Tennessee

Published by LifeWay Press® • © 2017 D. A. Horton

No part of this book may be reproduced or transmitted in any form or by any means, electronic or mechanical, including photocopying and recording, or by any information storage or retrieval system, except as may be expressly permitted in writing by the publisher. Requests for permission should be addressed in writing to LifeWay Press®; One LifeWay Plaza; Nashville, TN 37234-0152.

ISBN 978-1-4627-4208-0 • Item 005793179

Dewey decimal classification: 228
Subject headings: CHURCH \ BIBLE. N.T. REVELATION—
STUDY AND TEACHING \ END OF THE WORLD

Scripture quotations are taken from the Christian Standard Bible®, Copyright © 2017 by Holman Bible Publishers. Used by permission. Christian Standard Bible® and CSB® are federally registered trademarks of Holman Bible Publishers.

To order additional copies of this resource, write to LifeWay Resources Customer Service; One LifeWay Plaza; Nashville, TN 37234-0113; fax 615-251-5933; call toll free 800-458-2772; order online at lifeway.com; email orderentry@lifeway.com; or visit the LifeWay Christian Store serving you.

Printed in Canada

Groups Ministry Publishing • LifeWay Resources • One LifeWay Plaza • Nashville, TN 37234-0152

Contents

About the Authors

D. A. HORTON serves as the pastor of Reach Fellowship, a church plant in North Long Beach, California, and as the chief evangelist for the Urban Youth Workers Institute. Prior to his current roles, he served as an urban church planter/pastor in Kansas City, Missouri; a national coordinator of Urban Student Ministries at the North American Mission Board; and the executive director of ReachLife Ministries, a nonprofit ministry of Reach Records.

D. A. earned a bachelor of science in biblical studies from Calvary Bible College and a master's degree in Christian studies from Calvary Theological Seminary. He's currently working on a PhD in applied theology with a North American missions emphasis at Southeastern Baptist Theological Seminary.

D. A. is the author of *GOSPEL, DNA: Foundations of the Faith,* and *Bound to Be Free: Escaping Performance to Be Captured by Grace.* He and his wife, Elicia, have two daughters, Izabelle and Lola, and one son, D. A. Jr. (aka Duce).

BRANDON D. SMITH helped develop this Bible study. Brandon works with the Christian Standard Bible at LifeWay Christian Resources and teaches theology at various schools. The author of *Rooted: Theology for Growing Christians* and *They Spoke of Me: How Jesus Unlocks the Old Testament,* Brandon also cohosts the *Word Matters* podcast. He holds a BA in biblical studies from Dallas Baptist University and an MA in systematic and historical theology from Criswell College. He's pursuing a PhD in theology at Ridley College in Melbourne, Australia. Brandon lives near Nashville, Tennessee, with his wife, Christa, and their two daughters, Harper and Emma.

Introduction

Work. Sometimes we love it, sometimes we hate it, and sometimes we just get tried of loving it or hating it. We all work. Some of us work a regular job at a factory or an office. Some of us work at home. Some of us are students. Regardless, we all know that work is an inevitability in life.

The Bible defines works that are part of our life in Christ. Nothing we do can earn salvation; it's a gift from God. However, James 2:17 says, "Faith, if it doesn't have works, is dead by itself." In other words, although works can't bring salvation, once we're saved, our works show and prove our faith. And like our everyday work, our works in Christ are inevitable, and they have their ups and downs.

In Revelation 2–3 Jesus addressed the works of the seven churches in Asia Minor. Over the next six weeks we'll look at the ups and downs of those churches and draw out implications for our churches today:

Ephesus: The Church without Love
Smyrna: The Church That Was Persecuted
Pergamum and Thyatira: The Churches with Bad Reputations
Sardis: The Church That Fell Asleep
Philadelphia: The Church That Endured
Laodicea: The Church That Turned Lukewarm

My prayer is that we'll be honest with our small groups and ourselves as we look at the highs and lows of each church in Revelation. By digging deeply into the truths of Scripture, may we learn more about who we are and who Christ is for us. May we be the ones who conquer.

How to Use This Study

This Bible study book includes six weeks of content. Each week has an introductory page summarizing the focus of the week's study, followed by content designed for groups and individuals.

GROUP SESSIONS

Regardless of the day of the week your group meets, each week of content begins with the group session. This group session is designed to be one hour or more, with approximately 15 to 20 minutes of teaching and 45 minutes of personal interaction. It's even better if your group is able to meet longer than an hour, allowing more time for participants to interact with one another.

Each group session uses the following format to facilitate simple yet meaningful interaction among group members, with God's Word, and with the video teaching by D. A. Horton.

Start

This page includes questions to get the conversation started and to introduce the video segment.

Watch

This page includes key points from the video teaching, along with space for taking notes as participants watch the video.

Discuss

These two pages include questions and statements that guide the group to respond to the video teaching and to relevant Bible passages.

Pray

This final page of each group session includes a prompt for a closing time of prayer together and space for recording prayer requests of group members.

INDIVIDUAL DISCOVERY

Each *Disciple for Life* small-group resource provides individuals with optional activities during the week, appealing to different learning styles, schedules, and levels of engagement. These options include a plan for application and accountability, a Scripture-reading plan with journaling prompts, a devotion, and two personal studies. You can choose to take advantage of some or all of the options provided.

This Week's Plan

Immediately following the group session's prayer page is a weekly plan offering guidance for everyone to engage with that week's focal point, regardless of a person's maturity level or that week's schedule.

Read

A daily reading plan is outlined for Scriptures related to the group session. Space for personal notes is also provided. Instructions for using the HEAR journaling method for reading Scripture can be found on pages 8–11.

Reflect

A one-page devotional option is provided each week to help members reflect on a biblical truth related to the group session.

Personal Study

Two personal studies are provided each week to take individuals deeper into Scripture and to supplement the biblical truths introduced in the teaching time. These pages challenge individuals to grow in their understanding of God's Word and to make practical application to their lives.

LEADER GUIDE

Pages 120–31 at the back of this book contain a guide that develops a leader's understanding of the thought process behind questions and suggests ways to engage members at different levels of life-changing discussion.

The HEAR Journaling Method for Reading Scripture

Daily Bible Reading

Disciple for Life small-group Bible studies include a daily reading plan for each week. Making time in a busy schedule to focus on God through His Word is a vital part of the Christian life. If you're unable to do anything else provided in your Bible study book during a certain week, try to spend a few minutes in God's Word. The verse selections will take you deeper into stories and concepts that support the teaching and discussion during that week's group session.

Why Do You Need a Plan?

When you're a new believer or at various other times in your life, you may find yourself in a place where you don't know where to begin reading your Bible or how to personally approach Scripture. You may have tried the open-and-point method when you simply opened your Bible and pointed to a verse, hoping to get something out of the random selection from God's Word. Reading random Scriptures won't provide solid biblical growth any more then eating random food from your pantry will provide solid physical growth.

An effective plan must be well balanced for healthy growth. When it comes to reading the Bible, *well balanced* and *effective* mean reading and applying. A regular habit is great, but simply checking a box off your task list when you've completed your daily reading isn't enough. Knowing more about God is also great, but simply reading for spiritual knowledge still isn't enough. You also want to respond to what you're reading by taking action as you listen to what God is saying. After all, it's God's Word.

To digest more of the Word, *Disciple for Life* small-group Bible studies not only provide a weekly reading plan but also encourage you to use a simplified version of the HEAR journaling method. (If this method advances your personal growth, check out *Foundations: A 260-Day Bible-Reading Plan for Busy Believers* by Robby and Kandi Gallaty.)

Journaling What You HEAR in God's Word

You may or may not choose to keep a separate journal in addition to the space provided in this book. A separate journal would provide extra space as well as the opportunity to continue your journal after this study is completed. The HEAR journaling method promotes reading the Bible with a life-transforming purpose. You'll read in order to understand and respond to God's Word.

The HEAR acronym stands for *highlight, explain, apply,* and *respond.* Each of these four steps creates an atmosphere for hearing God speak. After settling on a reading plan, like the one provided in this book in the "Read" section each week, establish a time for studying God's Word. Then you'll be ready to HEAR from God.

Before You Begin: The Most Important Step

To really HEAR God speak to you through His Word, always begin your time with prayer. Pause and sincerely ask God to speak to you. It's absolutely imperative that you seek God's guidance in order to understand His Word (see 1 Cor. 2:12-14). Every time you open your Bible, pray a simple prayer like the one David prayed: "Open my eyes so that I may contemplate wondrous things from your instruction" (Ps. 119:18).

H = Highlight

After praying for the Holy Spirit's guidance, open this book to the week's reading plan, open a journal if you'd like more space than this book provides, and open your Bible. For an illustration let's assume you're reading Philippians 4:10-13. Verse 13 may jump out and speak to you as something you want to remember, so you'd simply highlight that verse in your Bible.

If keeping a HEAR journal, on the top line write the Scripture reference and the date and make up a title to summarize the meaning of the passage. Then write the letter H and record the verse that stood out and that you highlighted in your Bible. This practice will make it easy to look back through your journal to find a passage you want to revisit in the future.

E = Explain

After you've highlighted your verse(s), explain what the text means. Most simply, how would you summarize this passage in your own words? By asking some simple questions, with the help of God's Spirit, you can understand the meaning of the passage or verse. (A good study Bible can help answer more in-depth questions as you learn to explain a passage of Scripture.) Here are a few good questions to get you started:

- Why was the verse or passage written?
- To whom was it originally written?
- How does the verse or passage fit with the verses before and after it?
- Why would the Holy Spirit include this passage in the Bible book?
- What does God intend to communicate through the text?

If keeping a HEAR journal, below the H write the letter E and explain the text in your own words. Record any answers to questions that help you understand the passage of Scripture.

A = Apply

At this point you're beginning the process of discovering the specific personal word God has for you from His Word. What's important is that you're engaging with the text and wrestling with the meaning. Application is the heart of the process. Everything you've done so far coalesces under this heading. As you've done before, answer a series of questions to discover the significance of these verses to you personally, questions like:

- How can this verse or passage help me?
- What's God saying to me?
- What would the application of this verse look like in my life?

These questions bridge the gap between the ancient world and your world today. They provide a way for God to speak to you through the specific passage or verse.

If keeping a HEAR journal, write the letter A under the letter E, where you wrote a short summary explaining the text. Challenge yourself to write between two and five sentences about the way the text applies to your life.

R = Respond

Finally, you'll respond to the text. A personal response may take on many forms. You may write an action step to do, describe a change in perspective, or simply respond in prayer to what you've learned. For example, you may ask for help in being bold or generous, you may need to repent of unconfessed sin, or you may need to praise God. Keep in mind that you're responding to what you've just read.

In this book or in your journal, record your personal application of each passage of Scripture. You may want to write a brief explanation-and-application summary: "The verse means _____ , so I can or will _____."

If keeping a HEAR journal, write the letter R, along with the way you'll respond to what you highlighted, explained, and applied.

Notice that all the words in the HEAR method are action words: *highlight, explain, apply, respond.* God doesn't want us to sit back and wait for Him to drop truth into our laps. God wants us to actively pursue Him instead of waiting passively. Jesus said:

> Ask, and it will be given to you. Seek, and you will find.
> Knock, and the door will be opened to you.
> **Matthew 7:7**

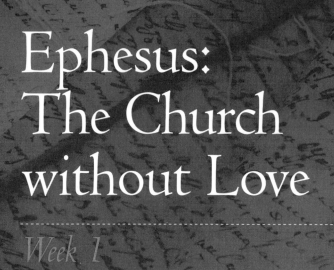

Ephesus:
The Church
without Love

Week 1

Sometimes we don't understand a movie until the end. Good storytellers take us on a journey, revealing a little at a time but not unveiling everything until the very end. Once we see the ending, the rest of the story makes sense. The Book of Revelation is a perfect example of this truth.

The apostle John wrote the seven letters recorded in Revelation 2–3 to specific churches in specific locations in ancient Asia Minor. These churches existed two thousand years ago, but the Storyteller—God Himself—gave them and us a glimpse into the future through His revelation to John. We know this because throughout the seven letters Jesus used the phrase "the one who conquers." Jesus used future tense to help the churches understand their present tense.

Our only hope to be conquerers is to look at Jesus, the One who conquered sin and death for us. In Him we can look out at our mission field—wherever that may be—with confidence, knowing we can conquer because of the victory given to us in Jesus' finished work on the cross.

We'll begin by looking at the church in Ephesus. The Ephesian Christians were excellent theologians. They stood firm against false doctrine and fake Christians, and their perseverance was apparently on point. Though the surface looked shiny, Jesus knew they were rotting from the inside; they had forgotten how to love. This was the loveless church.

When Jesus told the church that He's "the one who holds the seven stars in his right hand and who walks among the seven golden lampstands" (Rev. 2:1), He was telling them that He's intimately close to them. Jesus holds the entire church—the universal body of Christ—in His hand, and as He promised His disciples in Matthew 28:20, He's still with us. He was so near to the Ephesian believers that He could clearly see their outward works, and with perfect knowledge as God in the flesh, He could also see their hearts.

Start

Welcome everyone to session 1 of *Letters of the Revelation*. Use the following content to begin your group session together.

We mentioned in the introduction to this study that work is an inevitability in our daily lives, both as everyday citizens of this world and as believers in Christ. Through the letters to the seven churches in the Book of Revelation, we'll see again and again that Jesus noticed the works these churches were doing but almost always had corrections and promises for them.

Tell the group where you work and why you chose to work there.

Do you love what you do? Why or why not?

We often don't work from pure love for our jobs. Often we work to support our families or ourselves or to gain experience for a better job down the road. But even when we love our jobs, we can get bored with them after a few years of the daily grind. The truth is, anything can become familiar and grow stale, like a once-delicious loaf of bread.

We see this tendency in our own lives and in the lives of others. Successful athletes often retire, even when they have a few more years of tread on their tires, because they lose their love for the game. Sometimes friendships or relationships end because people struggle to love one another. We can even get tired of our favorite desserts!

In this session D. A. Horton will introduce us to Jesus' message to the church in Ephesus and will highlight the importance of renewing our love for Jesus.

Read Revelation 2:1-7 in preparation for the video and then watch video session 1.

Watch

Use the space below to follow along and take notes as you watch video session 1.

Realities in the Seven Letters

1. Jesus was actually speaking to seven literal churches that were in existence at the time of the giving of His revelation to the apostle John.
2. Jesus is actually speaking about how we can walk in the victory that He has secured for those who are part of the body of Christ.

Jesus' warnings to the seven churches in the Book of Revelation can give us hope and clarity regarding principles that we can apply so that we can be those who conquer in this life because of the victory that's been given to us through the precious blood of Jesus Christ.

Jesus is omniscient. He knows not only our words and our deeds. He has full, exhaustive knowledge of even our innermost thoughts that we never express to anybody else.

Corrections for the Church in Ephesus

1. Remember.

2. Repent.

3. Return.

The reward for loving your Savior with all you have is an eternal, uninterrupted, intimate fellowship with Him.

Discuss

Use the following statements and questions to discuss the video.

The most basic question we can ask when reading the letters of Revelation is "What's Jesus saying to me through these letters to the churches?" The beginning of the book helps us answer this question.

Read aloud Revelation 1:1-3.

As we see in this passage, this message is introduced as a revelation, an unveiling from God Himself through Jesus. As with all Scripture, God wants to tell us something directly through these words. If we heed these words, knowing Jesus could return at any moment, we'll be blessed (see v. 3).

In what ways have the words of Scripture recently taught you something about God? What did you learn?

How has reading God's Word helped you learn more about yourself?

How often would you say the impact of God's Word on your life in the past still influences the way you live for God today? Select one answer.

☐ Never
☐ Often
☐ Sometimes
☐ Always

D. A. said Jesus promises that we'll have victory in this life through the victory He achieved in His life, death, and resurrection. Specifically, the way to gain this victory is through rekindling our first love—the love we had for Jesus at first. This is the lesson Ephesus had to learn. The church was doing good works, but it was doing them with wrong motivations.

According to the video, what does it mean for Jesus to have full knowledge of our works?

Why is it important for Jesus not only to know our hearts but also to push us toward repentance?

D. A. used the example of marriage to demonstrate the importance of keeping our love fresh and alive. As Christ's bride, the church is called to listen to the voice of our Husband, who's calling us to keep our love for Him fresh and alive.

How do the acts of remembering and repenting help us keep our love for Jesus alive?

Why is it important not only to say we once loved and believed in Jesus but also to continually keep that love kindled?

What are your hopes or expectations for this study of the seven letters of Revelation?

May this week's study help us renew the love we had for Jesus when we first committed our lives to Him.

Conclude the group session with the prayer activity on the following page.

Pray

Conclude the group session with two actions.

1. Consider the group's responses to the truths of Scripture and pray for the Holy Spirit to work in our lives in the ways we've seen in God's Word.

   In what ways do you need to listen to God telling you to hear His words (see Rev. 1:3)?

   How will you think or act differently as a result of what God has revealed in His Word?

2. Pray for one another, particularly for God's help in applying the biblical truths studied and discussed during the group session. Ask God to reveal Himself and speak clearly to each person during the next six weeks.

Prayer Requests

Encourage members to complete "This Week's Plan" before the next group session.

This Week's Plan

Work with your group leader each week to create a plan for personal study, worship, and application between group sessions. Select from the following optional activities to match your personal preferences and available time.

Worship

[ ] Read your Bible. Complete the reading plan on page 20.

[ ] Spend time with God by engaging with the devotional experience on page 21.

[ ] Connect with God every day in prayer.

Personal Study

[ ] Read and interact with "Work, Work, Work" on page 22.

[ ] Read and interact with "Rekindled Love" on page 26.

Application

[ ] Memorize Revelation 2:4-5.

[ ] Identify someone in your life who'll speak the truth and help you fight the temptation to grow cold against God.

[ ] Connect over coffee with someone in the group. Discuss your thoughts on this week's study and your expectations for the group going forward.

[ ] Start a journal. This week record at least five ways you try to earn God's love through works. Then pray that God will help you rest in His unearned grace.

Did you miss the group session?
Video sessions available for purchase at lifeway.com/revelation

19

Read

Read the following Scripture passages this week. Use the acronym HEAR and the space provided to record your thoughts or action steps.

Day 1: Revelation 1

Day 2: Revelation 2:1-7

Day 3: James 2:14-18

Day 4: Mark 12:28-34

Day 5: Hebrews 11

Day 6: 1 Corinthians 13

Day 7: Revelation 21–22

Reflect

SERVE FROM A HEART OF LOVE

Any good leader will tell you it's important for employees not only to do their jobs well but also to have a passion for what they do, for the people they do it with, and for the people they do it for. The best employees clock in and out each day for more than a paycheck. They spend their workdays advancing the goals and the mission of their employers.

In a similar way, God desires that we serve from a heart of love. He wants us to love the mission to which He calls us, not just stay busy working. Read these words by the apostle Paul:

> If I speak human or angelic tongues but do not have love, I am a noisy gong or a clanging cymbal. If I have the gift of prophecy and understand all mysteries and all knowledge, and if I have all faith so that I can move mountains but do not have love, I am nothing. And if I give away all my possessions, and if I give over my body in order to boast but do not have love, I gain nothing.
> **1 Corinthians 13:1-3**

In this passage Paul said when we serve without love, we say nothing, we are nothing, and we gain nothing. Everything we do must come from genuine love—for God and for others. We serve not from obligation, satisfaction, or recognition but because of the great love God has demonstrated to us.

Read 1 John 3:16-18 and reflect on the questions that follow.

How has God's love for you shaped your love for Him?

How does this love shape the way you serve God and others?

Personal Study 1

WORK, WORK, WORK

"Get saved and then get to work." This phrase is said either explicitly or implicitly in many churches. Once people place their faith in Christ, they're often given a list of rules—works—to follow. Read the Bible. Pray. Go to church gatherings on Sundays. Volunteer. You know the drill. Get to work, and when you're tired, work some more. But surely there's more to following Jesus than a to-do list.

From the onset of the letter to the Ephesian church in Revelation 2, it seems that the Ephesians were doing all the right things—seeking to live in purity, rebuking false teachers, and laboring through hardship. Jesus even commended the believers for these things. Paul's beautiful letter to the Ephesians, decades before this was written, likely laid a deep foundation for their theology and identity. They knew right from wrong, and they knew how to work hard for the Kingdom. Read Jesus' words to the church:

> Write to the angel of the church in Ephesus: Thus says the one who holds the seven stars in his right hand and who walks among the seven golden lampstands: I know your works, your labor, and your endurance, and that you cannot tolerate evil people. You have tested those who call themselves apostles and are not, and you have found them to be liars. I know that you have persevered and endured hardships for the sake of my name, and have not grown weary. But I have this against you: You have abandoned the love you had at first. Remember then how far you have fallen; repent, and do the works you did at first. Otherwise, I will come to you and remove your lampstand from its place, unless you repent. Yet you do have this: You hate the practices of the Nicolaitans, which I also hate. Let anyone who has ears to hear listen to what the Spirit says to the churches. To the one who conquers, I will give the right to eat from the tree of life, which is in the paradise of God.
> **Revelation 2:1-7**

Notice that Jesus included both compliments and rebukes. He praised them for their strong doctrine, their defense of the faith, and their good ethics. Although Jesus was sincere in these compliments, the Ephesian believers were by no means perfect. They were practically running a theological training school—let's call it the first seminary (see Acts 19:8-10)—and they were standing firm against cultural pressures, but their love for Jesus had grown cold. They focused on the important work they were doing but forgot why they were doing it.

Read these words about Kingdom work from the Book of James:

> What good is it, my brothers and sisters, if someone claims to have faith but does not have works? Can such faith save him? If a brother or sister is without clothes and lacks daily food and one of you says to them, "Go in peace, stay warm, and be well fed," but you don't give them what the body needs, what good is it? In the same way faith, if it doesn't have works, is dead by itself. But someone will say, "You have faith, and I have works." Show me your faith without works, and I will show you faith by my works. You believe that God is one. Good! Even the demons believe—and they shudder.
> **James 2:14-19**

In this passage circle the words *faith* and *works* every time they appear. Then underline the questions James asked.

Record the pattern you notice in these words and questions. What response was James trying to elicit from his readers?

James was telling his audience that simply believing God is real doesn't save anyone. Even Satan and his demons know God exists. James took it a step further, saying works are an integral part of showing and proving that we truly love God. Want to know whether your faith is legitimate? Compare it to the command Jesus said is the greatest:

> Love the Lord your God with all your heart, with all your soul, with all your
> mind, and with all your strength. … Love your neighbor as yourself.
> **Mark 12:30-31**

This was the question the Ephesians needed to answer. Did they love God with their hearts and souls or just with their minds and strength? Jesus would provide the answer. He was so intimately near and involved in the lives of the Ephesians that He was able to say, "I know your works, your labor, and your endurance" (Rev. 2:2). Right off the bat, we see that these brothers and sisters got to work. It would be hard to say they had no faith if we merely looked at all the shiny fruit hanging from the vine. But Jesus sees the roots too. He sees our work for what it is—good (motivated by love) and bad (motivated by performance).

If you looked at your own life, what might Jesus find commendable about your works?

In what ways do you think your work for God demonstrates a lack of love for Him?

This is a busy congregation; they were doing a lot of work to defend the Christian faith and to maintain external purity. They toiled through hardship and maintained their endurance—finishing the work they set out to do.

Jesus also commended the church for their good theology and willingness to remove false teachers from the congregation. Like Jesus, they hated "the practices of the Nicolaitans" (v. 6). Not much is known about the Nicolaitans, but some early Christian sources link them to sexual sin and eating meat sacrificed to idols. They were people who claimed to be Christians but abused God's grace. Their works weren't from faith but from their desire to indulge in sin. The Ephesians didn't tolerate the Nicolaitans' hypocrisy.

Are you comfortable recognizing and calling out sin in others' lives? In what ways can confronting sins in others be beneficial?

No doubt it can be good to recognize sins in others. In 1 Corinthians 5 Paul scolded the church for allowing someone to walk around in sin unchallenged. He even went so far as to recommend that they kick the man out of the church. The Ephesians followed Paul's actions with the Nicolaitans. Yet the Ephesians didn't recognize their own hypocrisy. They had become programmed machines, going through the motions but disconnected from the reason they existed in the first place. They knew the right doctrine but struggled to love the God they were created to work for.

Because we're all created in God's image, our good deeds are truly useful only if they're connected to His holy character. Yes, faith without works is dead, but works without living faith in God are also worthless:

> Now without faith it is impossible to please God, since the one who draws near to him must believe that he exists and that he rewards those who seek him.
> **Hebrews 11:6**

List any ways your fire for God has dimmed since you first placed your faith in Christ.

Jesus pointed out that works are good as long as they're truly motivated by faith and love. The Ephesians' works, however, were ultimately motivated by something other than love. Yet Jesus didn't leave the Ephesians, and He won't leave us. As we'll see, He provides us with grace and encouragement to love Him passionately, and He promises that we'll live in His grace for eternity.

Close your study time in prayer, asking God to help you serve Him and others from genuine love for Jesus.

Personal Study 2

REKINDLED LOVE

In personal study 1 we looked at Jesus' words about the works of the Ephesians. On the one hand, they were doing good things for the Kingdom—protecting truth and persevering in difficult times. On the other hand, however, their works were missing something important—love (see Rev. 2.4).

Jesus could have stopped with the compliments. He could have been happy with the Ephesians' good works. But He didn't stop there, because their works weren't coming from the right motivation.

> **Why was Jesus' one critique more important than the several positive qualities about the Ephesian church?**

> **Why did Jesus want the Ephesians not only to do good works but also to remember their love for Him?**

> **In what areas of your life are you most prone to be motivated by something other than your love for Christ?**

Years before Jesus spoke this message to the Ephesian church, Paul had warned them not to forget why they did good works:

> You are saved by grace through faith, and this is not from yourselves; it is God's gift—not from works, so that no one can boast. For we are his workmanship, created in Christ Jesus for good works, which God prepared ahead of time for us to do.
> **Ephesians 2:8-10**

Paul told the church in Ephesus that good works are a result of our faith in Christ. We're created to do good works for His glory, not our own. If we do good works for our own benefit, they lose their power. But if we do them because of our love for Christ, they reveal the gospel's power.

Why is it powerful to think about our works as something God has already "prepared ahead of time for us to do" (v. 10)?

List ways this truth changes the way you view your works in Christ.

Jesus didn't just tell the Ephesians to return to their love for Him. He told them how to do it:

> Remember then how far you have fallen; repent, and do
> the works you did at first. Otherwise, I will come to you and
> remove your lampstand from its place, unless you repent.
> **Revelation 2:5**

When my wife and I were preparing for marriage, we often talked about planting a church and living our lives on mission together. We poured much of our lives into our plans. Over time the mission became bigger than our love for each other. In the same way, Christ's bride, the church, can focus on mission so much that our love for Him grows dim. Thankfully, Jesus gave us two ways to renew our love for Him.

First, Jesus told the Ephesians to remember. Many times in Scripture, God reminded His children about the works He had done for them. Reflecting on God's faithfulness in our lives strengthens our love for Him. When the Ephesians reflected on the love they had for Jesus at first, they would be able to see all He had done in them and for them.

Second, Jesus told the Ephesians to repent. If they didn't, they would have their lampstand removed; they would no longer shine light on Ephesus as Christ's representatives. To repent is to turn away from sin and turn our eyes back on Christ—to return to the fundamentals of following Him. The only chance the Ephesians had of returning to their love for Jesus and of continuing their ministry in Ephesus was to remember Him and rely on Him.

Look back on your life and list ways God has been faithful to you. Who in your life can help you regularly remember and repent?

As the letter to the church in Ephesus concluded, Jesus promised:

Let anyone who has ears to hear listen to what the Spirit says to the churches. To the one who conquers, I will give the right to eat from the tree of life, which is in the paradise of God.
Revelation 2:7

Jesus told the Ephesians what would happen if they returned to their first love. The promise Jesus made is powerful, even for churches today: those who conquer—who win the fight against a stale, loveless faith—will be given "the right to eat from the tree of life, which is in the paradise of God." This tree of life shows up in two other key places in Scripture:

The LORD God said, "Since the man has become like one of us, knowing good and evil, he must not reach out, take from the tree of life, eat, and live forever." So the LORD God sent him away from the garden of Eden to work the ground from which he was taken.
Genesis 3:22-23

The tree of life was on each side of the river, bearing twelve kinds of fruit, producing its fruit every month. The leaves of the tree are for healing the nations, and there will no longer be any curse. The throne of God and of the Lamb will be in the city, and his servants will worship him.
Revelation 22:2-3

The tree of life was in the middle of the garden of Eden before sin entered the world (see Gen. 2:9). When Adam and Even disobeyed God and introduced sin into the world, they lost their access to the tree of life because the consequence of sin isn't life but death (see Rom. 6:23). Yet after Christ returns and destroys sin and death, God's people will once again have access to the tree of life. One day God will return the world to the way it was in the garden of Eden—but even better. We'll feast on the fruit of the tree of life for eternity.

Identify stark differences between God's relationship with people in Genesis 3 and with people in Revelation 22.

The church in Ephesus was at a crossroads. If they returned to their love for Christ, their doors would remain open, and the light would shine out; if they continued working without a supreme love for Jesus, their doors would close. The point is simple: if you love your ministry, theology, or good deeds more than Christ, you've lost your first love and need to repent.

Right now we're still under the curse of Adam and Eve, so the tree of life isn't available to us, and death is still inevitable. However, Jesus told the Ephesians and us that maintaining a passionate love for Him will allow us to eat from the tree of life for eternity. For those who love Christ, the promise of Revelation 22 is still available. May we remind not only ourselves but also the whole world of this glorious truth.

Close your study time in prayer, asking God to keep your passion for Jesus burning brightly.

Smyrna:
The Church That
Was Persecuted

It's easy to feel persecuted in our culture today. Sometimes the courts don't go the way we want them to. Sometimes our faith comes into conflict with the culture around us. And sometimes we face direct persecution—physical, emotional, or legal distress because of our love for Jesus.

It's easy to allow the culture to have its way. If we bow down in the face of persecution or trouble, we might get off easier. Sometimes submitting to an earthly king instead of the King of kings appears to bring relief. Other times it seems easier to cheat our employers or loved ones in order to get ahead. But in reality, only the King of kings can give us true rest.

The city of Smyrna had a history of distress. Whether through military invasion or natural disaster, Smyrna knew hard times. Many citizens worshiped false gods, thinking this would enable them to recuperate from the previous disaster and be spared from the next. Others bowed down to the Roman emperor, hoping to gain immediate reprieve.

The church in Smyrna faced even more difficulty. They were ridiculed and mocked for their faith. But Jesus told the church in Smyrna to look to Him, the One whose resurrection would give them resurrection. The persecution they faced was difficult, yes, but not impossible to endure. Because of Jesus they were rich in poverty and would have life in death.

Jesus told the believers in Smyrna that even though Satan himself would come against them, they must "be faithful to the point of death," and Jesus would give them "the crown of life" (Rev. 2:10). No affliction a believer faces can overwhelm the victory we have through Christ's death and resurrection.

Start

....

Welcome everyone to session 2 of *Letters of the Revelation*. Use the following content to begin your group session together.

In the previous group session we were asked to remember God's faithfulness to us and to repent of ways we've turned our hearts to something or someone other than Jesus.

> As you spent time in God's Word and prayer this week, in what ways did God show you that you weren't loving Him wholeheartedly?

> Did you take any steps of faith in response to this revelation? If so, what did you do? If not, why not?

> From your personal study in week 1, what were some key truths you learned about renewing your love for Jesus?

This week we'll learn that God calls us to put away easy comfort and accept Jesus' promise that all afflictions in this life are momentary. We'll see that Jesus' resurrection is more powerful than any temptation to give in to internal or external pressure. Let's watch as D. A. tells us more about Jesus' words to the church in Smyrna.

Read Revelation 2:8-11 in preparation for the video and then watch video session 2.

Watch

Use the space below to follow along and take notes as you watch video session 2.

Jesus is telling us, "I will reward you with life everlasting if you will continue to deny the pagan practices of the society around you and allow Myself to be the One who gives you all the prosperity that is necessary spiritually, whether it comes physically through material gain or not."

Am I willing to crucify my flesh? Am I willing to say no to the misdeeds of my flesh, through the empowerment of the indwelling of God the Holy Spirit, in order to pursue holiness throughout the mundane activities of everyday life?

God the Holy Spirit lives inside every Christian. He gives us the strength to put to death the misdeeds of our flesh so that we can say no to our flesh and yes to the things of God.

We took God's plan of redemption when we admitted we were sinners, and we embraced Christ as our Lord and Savior.

Live like you have eternal life. Eternal life does not begin when we enter glory. Eternal life begins the moment of our conversion.

Discuss

Use the following statements and questions to discuss the video.

D. A. began by pointing out the way Jesus opened His letter to the church in Smyrna.

Read aloud Revelation 2:8.

Jesus told these believers that He's "the First and the Last, the one who was dead and came to life." That's quite a name! This name tells us two important facts about Jesus:

1. Jesus is the First and the Last. In other words, He's eternal. Because He's God in the flesh, He lives forever.

2. Jesus was once dead and then came to life. This point is directly tied to the previous one. Because Jesus came to earth in the flesh, He could die as a man, but because He was God, death didn't have the last word.

   Why is it important to understand that Jesus wasn't merely a man but God in the flesh?

   Why would Jesus introduce Himself this way to a church that was suffering persecution?

The church in Smyrna was hurting. Their neighbors slandered them, and Satan himself attacked them. If they're anything like us, they likely struggled to trust that God was really present with them.

   Identify a time in your life when you were slandered or attacked.

   How did you respond to God? Were you quick to praise Him for your suffering, did you try to fix it on your own, or did you get angry at God?

Let's consider the way D. A. contrasted the resurrection story of Smyrna's people and the resurrection story of Jesus:

- The citizens of Smyrna gathered to ask false gods to resurrect their city.

- Jesus told the church in Smyrna to look to His resurrection as the only resurrection story worth celebrating.

  What are some major differences between these two stories?

  Why does Jesus' story offer a better hope than Smyrna's story?

  In what ways have you believed the lies of a false resurrection story instead of trusting in Jesus' resurrection?

The world tells us that we can resurrect ourselves in times of trouble or that we can look to an entity like the government to save us. But Jesus said His kingdom, brought by His coming, is the only kingdom in which we can place our hope. In His resurrection we have hope for our own resurrection (see 1 Cor. 15).

  How does Jesus' resurrection encourage believers in times of suffering or persecution?

  How can your community of friends and family help point you to the power of Jesus' resurrection?

Conclude the group session with the prayer activity on the following page.

Pray

Conclude the group session with two actions.

1. Consider the group's responses to the truths of Scripture and pray for the Holy Spirit to work in our lives in the ways we've seen in God's Word.

   In what ways can you help yourself remember and believe the peace found in Jesus' resurrection during spiritual attacks and persecution?

   How will you think or act differently as a result of what God has revealed in His Word?

2. Pray for one another, particularly for God's help in applying the biblical truths studied and discussed during the group session.

Spend a few minutes praying for each person in the group. Ask God to reveal Himself and speak clearly to each person this week.

Prayer Requests

Encourage members to complete "This Week's Plan" before the next group session.

This Week's Plan

Work with your group leader each week to create a plan for personal study, worship, and application between group sessions. Select from the following optional activities to match your personal preferences and available time.

Worship

[ ] Read your Bible. Complete the reading plan on page 38.

[ ] Spend time with God by engaging with the devotional experience on page 39.

[ ] Connect with God every day in prayer.

Personal Study

[ ] Read and interact with "Resisting Pressure" on page 40.

[ ] Read and interact with "Embracing Suffering" on page 44.

Application

[ ] Memorize Revelation 2:10c.

[ ] Identify someone who can speak the truth and help you fight the temptation to let suffering point you toward anything but God.

[ ] Connect over coffee with someone in the group. Discuss your thoughts on this week's study and your expectations for the group going forward.

[ ] Continue your journal. This week record at least five ways you can remember Jesus' resurrection in times of suffering, struggles, or frustration.

Did you miss the group session?
Video sessions available for purchase at lifeway.com/revelation

37

Read

Read the following Scripture passages this week. Use the acronym HEAR and the space provided to record your thoughts or action steps.

Day 1: Revelation 2:8-11

Day 2: Ephesians 1:3-14

Day 3: Hebrews 2:5-18

Day 4: 2 Corinthians 4:7-18

Day 5: Hebrews 12:1-13

Day 6: 1 Corinthians 15

Day 7: Mark 8:31-38

Reflect

GROANING TOGETHER

Our culture is fixated on the here and now. We can order food, books, or movies in just a few minutes without leaving our couches. It's easier than ever to make life easier than ever. We're so accustomed to ease that a micro-wave—once a marvelous invention of convenience—can make us impatient if it doesn't heat our leftovers quickly enough.

One by-product of our instant-gratification culture is that we've come to view life through a me-centered, get-what-I-can-when-I-can lens. It's difficult to sit and wait. It's more difficult to patiently endure pain and suffering. But the world wasn't originally intended to frustrate us. Frustration and futility came with the curse when Adam and Eve committed the first sin:

> The ground is cursed because of you.
> You will eat from it by means of painful labor
> all the days of your life.
> It will produce thorns and thistles for you,
> and you will eat the plants of the field.
> You will eat bread by the sweat of your brow
> until you return to the ground,
> since you were taken from it.
> For you are dust,
> and you will return to dust.
> **Genesis 3:17-19**

As a result of the curse, even "creation has been groaning together" (Rom. 8:22), waiting for redemption. But as ministers of reconciliation (see 2 Cor 5:18), we're called to rise above our fallen nature and remain faithful to Christ. We mourn but not as people who have no hope (see I Thess. 4:13). Temporary trials are meant to strengthen us, not to discourage us, because we know God is "making everything new" (Rev. 21:5).

Personal Study 1

RESISTING PRESSURE

We've all heard the story of someone who wanted to get ahead at work. He slaved away at his job, hoping to get a promotion or a raise. His boss didn't notice. His coworkers didn't vouch for him. So feeling underappreciated and overworked, he began to cheat. Before long he was caught up in a web of lies. He was inflating his numbers and exaggerating his successes, claiming he had made bigger deals and better sales than he actually had. And he had become so entangled in the web that he was unable to escape.

We can all be tempted to buckle under the weight of cultural, corporate, or relational pressure. We want to be respected and loved. And some people are willing to commit just about any immoral act to gain that success or approval.

> **To which of these temptations are you most susceptible to give in?**
> ☐ **Seeking others' approval**
> ☐ **Getting ahead at school, work, sports, and so on**
> ☐ **Avoiding conflict**
>
> **Identify a situation in which you felt pressured to compromise biblical principles. How did you respond?**

The saints in Smyrna no doubt felt pressure to give in to persecution and ridicule. It must have been weighty. Like all of us, they may have felt tempted to compromise their beliefs in order to gain temporal, immediate relief. That's why Jesus encouraged the church in Smyrna to hold fast to Him:

> Write to the angel of the church in Smyrna: Thus says the First and the
> Last, the one who was dead and came to life: I know your affliction and
> poverty, but you are rich. I know the slander of those who say they are
> Jews and are not, but are a synagogue of Satan. Don't be afraid of what

you are about to suffer. Look, the devil is about to throw some of you into prison to test you, and you will experience affliction for ten days. Be faithful to the point of death, and I will give you the crown of life. Let anyone who has ears to hear listen to what the Spirit says to the churches. The one who conquers will never be harmed by the second death.

Revelation 2:8-11

In the previous passage circle all the times Jesus encouraged the saints in Smyrna. In what ways are these encouragements better than the pressures the church faced?

It's an age-old lie—all the way back to the first sin, in fact—to believe God simply isn't enough. Sometimes He feels distant or detached, as though He might come to our rescue in the end, but in this life we need to grit our teeth and try to get by. That's the way Satan temped Adam and Eve:

The woman said to the serpent, "We may eat the fruit from the trees in the garden. But about the fruit of the tree in the middle of the garden, God said, 'You must not eat it or touch it, or you will die.' " "No! You will not die," the serpent said to the woman. "In fact, God knows that when you eat it your eyes will be opened and you will be like God, knowing good and evil." The woman saw that the tree was good for food and delightful to look at, and that it was desirable for obtaining wisdom. So she took some of its fruit and ate it; she also gave some to her husband, who was with her, and he ate it.

Genesis 3:2-6

In the first pressure to disobey God, Adam and Eve gave in. They thought God was holding out on them, so they traded their eternal lives for a momentary bite of fruit. The sweet juice from the fruit quickly became a bitter pill. That one act, that one submission to pressure, caused a monumental rift in their relationship with each other and with God.

When have you felt that God was the distant? How did you respond?

Even though Jesus told us that He would be with us forever (see Matt. 28:20), why do we feel at times that He's distant?

How do Jesus' words in Revelation 2:8-11 change the way we think about His intimate interest in our lives?

We like to think we would have responded differently than Adam and Eve did: "If I had been there, I would have told Satan to get lost!" But as children of Adam, we must acknowledge that we're no different from him (see Rom. 5:12). Like the church in Smyrna, we need to continually remind ourselves to turn our eyes away from the antigospel story that leads to death and fix our eyes on the risen Jesus and the true gospel story of redemption.

We can see the true gospel in the way Jesus contrasted Himself with the false gods of the day. Smyrna was known for its worship of false gods. The goddess Cybele, known as the mother of the gods, was worshiped alongside Zeus and Caesar. Every spring Cybele was credited for the rebirth of nature alongside the mythological resurrection of her lover, Attis. When an earthquake hit, the people of Smyrna called out for these gods to restore their land.

When Jesus called Himself "the First and the Last, the one who was dead and came to life" (Rev. 2:8), He was reminding the saints in Smyrna that He alone was alive before all false gods, and He alone would be alive after the reputations of all false gods faded. Furthermore, His resurrection, which provides eternal life for all saints, releases us from death and assures us that one day Jesus will restore all things—our bodies, our souls, and creation itself (see Rev. 21–22).

Why would the people of Smyrna be tempted to turn toward false gods for assurance in their circumstances?

How does Jesus' description of Himself in Revelation 2:8 shape the way we view false gods, temptations, and Satan?

How does our future hope of final redemption affect our lives now?

Notice that Jesus didn't rebuke the church in Smyrna. Instead, he encouraged them not to fear and to persevere. He told them in verse 9 that though they were materially poor, their perseverance would make them spiritually rich. Worse persecution was coming from Satan in the form of imprisonment, but even their deaths would bring them eternal life. The second death (see v. 11) is the final word for those who don't place their faith in Christ, but Jesus' word of eternal life conquers even the second death.

I'd like to think I would never abandon the gospel, even if threatened with imprisonment. I want to believe I would never recant the gospel, regardless of the situation. No one knows what persecution Christians might face in the future, but Jesus' words to the church in Smyrna can prepare us today.

Every four years we're tempted to put our hope in a candidate's promise of peace. At our jobs we're tempted to cut corners to get ahead. We may even be willing to lie if it means avoiding a challenging conversation or getting approval.

Jesus' resurrection frees us from these lies. His story tells us that cultural, political, and relational pressures are fleeting. If we give in to them, we may find momentary comfort, but we may sacrifice much more: spiritual wealth and eternal life. In Christ we have "every spiritual blessing in the heavens" (Eph. 1:3). We don't need anything more.

Personal Study 2

EMBRACING SUFFERING

In the previous study we talked about the pressure to conform to ungodliness in order to avoid persecution. The church in Smyrna wasn't merely facing pressure from outsiders; they were looking down the barrel at actual suffering. It seems as if they were tempted not only to conform but also to deny Christ in order to stay out of prison or worse.

We hear of intense persecution and suffering overseas—Christians martyred for their faith, unable to feed their families because their community ostracizes them, or too poor to have clean water or a roof over their heads. Yet they hold on to their faith.

Put yourself in their shoes. Imagine you're on your knees in front a man who is about to kill you for your faith. Imagine someone offers you a job or enough money that you'll never have to worry about starvation again. Imagine someone offers you clean water or a medication to cure your illness. However, the only way you can be rescued is to deny Christ and turn away from the Christian faith.

The church in Smyrna faced that kind of persecution. Slandered and mocked by others and facing potential imprisonment, they would have found it easy to say, "Christian? I'm not a Christian!" This might have stopped the attacks and made life easier for a while. But Jesus told them, "Don't be afraid of what you are about to suffer" (Rev. 2:10).

Have you ever been in a situation in which you were pressured to deny Christ? What did you say or do?

In what ways does Jesus offer believers comfort in these situations?

When Jesus said the church in Smyrna shouldn't fear their upcoming persecution, He was making them aware of what was going to happen to them. As God in the flesh, He knew what was coming for them. But He told them to remain faithful even when persecution came: "Be faithful to the point of death" (v. 10).

Job faced a similar situation. God allowed Satan to throw everything he had at Job. Satan bet that Job would deny God, but God knew Job would remain faithful. Job lost his family, his livelihood, and his physical health. He was understandably frustrated, but he never wavered:

> Job stood up, tore his robe, and shaved his head.
> He fell to the ground and worshiped, saying:
>> Naked I came from my mother's womb,
>> and naked I will leave this life.
>> The LORD gives, and the LORD takes away.
>> Blessed be the name of the LORD.
> Throughout all this Job did not sin or blame God for anything.
> **Job 1:20-22**

Job wasn't facing daily inconveniences we encounter today, like fighting traffic, spilling our coffee, or mishandling an argument. Job lost everything and then some. He wasn't imprisoned, but he was definitely under siege.

The church in Smyrna faced the same temptation as Job, and Jesus essentially told them to respond the same way Job did. He instructed them to rely on the Lord and not to give in to the temptation of their flesh either to blame

God or to turn to something more comfortable. He told them to look to His victorious resurrection (see Rev. 2:8), which makes any suffering we experience in this life a "momentary light affliction" (2 Cor. 4:17), as Paul described it.

> **In what ways does the suffering of the church in Smyrna and the suffering of Job give us comfort in our own suffering or even in everyday inconveniences?**

Believers today might think they can't relate to the church in Smyrna because Christians in America aren't facing imprisonment or death for their faith, at least not normally, at a cultural or governmental level. Nevertheless, we face suffering every day. Work can feel meaningless. Our marriages aren't always candy and roses. Our bodies break down. Family members or friends get sick. Relationships go bad. And in very real ways, we can be targeted for our faith. We all suffer the effects of living in a broken world.

Jesus promised if the church in Smyrna was "faithful to the point of death," He would give them "the crown of life" (Rev. 2:10). Smyrna was called the crown of Asia Minor because of the city's beauty. Every year Smyrna's rulers were presented with a crown of leaves for their faithfulness in governing the city. Jesus reminded the saints in Smyrna that He would give them the crown of life for their faithfulness to Him, but it may come with great suffering—even death.

> **What's your reaction to this phrase in verse 10: "Be faithful to the point of death"? How does it make you think about your own faithfulness to God?**

No one can bestow on us a better crown than the crown of eternal life with God. There's no greater victory. We'll know no greater joy, and all suffering in this life will seem small compared to it. In this life we may be mocked or persecuted, but we'll reign forever with Christ as kings and queens of the universe (see Rev. 20:4-6). One day God will end suffering once and for all, and we can live in anticipation of that glorious time (see 21:1-5).

Why will Christians receive a crown for suffering well?

Describe some ways God uses suffering in the lives of His children.

Read 1 Corinthians 15:12-22. How does the resurrection of Christ provide hope for believers who suffer?

The hope we have because of Jesus' resurrection wasn't meant only for the church in Smyrna, and it's not meant only for us. This letter proclaims to the world that Jesus' resurrection story is better than any story the world can tell. Death is every person's enemy, yet Jesus has already tasted death for us (see Heb. 2:9). We can embrace suffering because Christ first embraced it for us. And because He was resurrected, we'll be resurrected also. Because of His victory over sin and death, our victory is guaranteed.

We can take the message to the world that this life isn't the end. It's only the beginning. No matter how much we may suffer, our future is secure in Christ. In this life suffering is guaranteed, but it won't last. This is good news in a bad-news world.

Pergamum and Thyatira: The Churches with Bad Reputations

Week 3

Discipline is hard. As kids, we all dreaded it. If you have kids now, you know how much they dread it.

But as parents, we know right discipline is meant to grow our kids into the image of Christ. We want to shape their morals so that they'll become godly adults. We want to explain their errors to them so that they'll learn to make right decisions. We want to explain the gospel to them so that their worldview won't be poisoned by false gospels.

In Revelation 2 Jesus had discipline and warnings for the churches in Pergamum and Thyatira. Their reputations preceded them: they faced persecution well, and they loved others well. But Jesus warned them that their worldview was skewed. Their confession of the gospel was strong, but their practices didn't quite match up. They were abusing God's grace by dabbling in false worship. They thought their freedom in Christ gave them license to sin.

Jesus told these saints that He wouldn't tolerate their ongoing rebellion. They couldn't maintain two allegiances and expect forgiveness. Instead, they should repent and accept His offer of life-giving manna as opposed to meat sacrificed to false gods. Although these churches were free from condemnation, they weren't free from discipline.

Jesus wants a pure, spotless bride. He won't stand by and watch His church stain herself with ongoing sin.

Start

In the previous group session we were encouraged to accept the inevitability of suffering, while finding comfort in Jesus' victory over sin and death.

> **As you spent time in God's Word and prayer this week, in what ways did God show you ways you were tempted to compromise your faith in Christ in order to avoid suffering?**

> **Did you take any steps of faith in response to this revelation? If so, what did you do? If not, why not?**

> **List some ways you can obey God's call to a radical faith that doesn't back down in the face of persecution.**

In this session we'll learn that God wants Christians not only to withstand cultural pressures and persecution but also to take seriously His call to repent of ongoing sin in our lives. Because Jesus takes sin seriously, He wants us to continually repent in order to walk in truth and become more like Him. In this video session D. A. will tell us more about Jesus' warnings to the churches in Pergamum and Thyatira.

Read Revelation 2:12-29 in preparation for the video and then watch video session 3.

Watch

Use the space below to follow along and take notes as you watch video session 3.

Jesus Christ rules with righteousness, and He pronounces judgment with full authority.

The story of martyrs actually fuels the faith of Christians who remain alive.

It's one thing to say, "I'll die for Christ," but Jesus is saying, "Saints, will you live for Me?"

You will have uninterrupted, eternal fellowship with Him by staying faithful, rejecting compromise, and conquering and walking in the victory that Jesus Christ has secured for His bride, the church. He will give to you, as your reward, Himself.

Jesus is serious about corruption in His church.

Discuss

Use the following statements and questions to discuss the video.

D. A. taught that applying God's Word to our lives and to our churches is crucial in fighting the temptations of compromise and corruption. In fact, he encouraged us to "walk in victory over compromise and corruption by looking at the Word of God, placing our hearts in submission to its authority and in submission to the local church leaders who are biblically qualified to serve us in that position."

What are some areas of compromise and corruption you see in your life?

Why is it crucial to identify sin in our lives and churches?

How does Jesus ultimately give us victory over compromise and corruption?

Read aloud Matthew 18:15-20.

In this passage Jesus instructs us in how to handle conflict with our brothers and sisters in Christ. Christians should never live on a spiritual island. Instead, we should seek to repent to God and to one another, and we should be willing to address sins in one another's lives.

Why is it easy to notice sins in others' lives but not in our own hearts?

What are the greatest reasons we hesitate to repent of our own sins?

What are the greatest reasons we hesitate to confront others' sins?

God's discipline is brought about by love. He wants to conform us to the image of Christ. Likewise, when we confront one another's sins, we should do so in love. When we give and receive correction in godly love, seeking to help one another become more like Christ, we faithfully follow Jesus' model in Matthew 18.

Why does Jesus encourage us to bring along witnesses when we confront another believer's sin?

Why is Jesus' promise to be among us at those times so important?

The account before Jesus' outline for church discipline discusses a shepherd's desire to find a lost sheep (see vv. 12-13), and the following account discusses an unforgiving servant (see vv. 21-35). Considering all these teachings, we learn two key truths:

1. God wants all people to be restored and conformed to the image of Christ.

2. Forgiving one another shows our understanding of God's forgiveness for us.

What can we learn about forgiveness from God's sending of Jesus to earth and from Jesus' death on the cross?

How can your group create and build a culture of discipline that's rooted in the gospel?

Conclude the group session with the prayer activity on the following page.

Pray

Conclude the group session with two actions.

I. Consider the group's responses to the truths of Scripture and pray for the Holy Spirit to work in our lives in the ways we've seen in God's Word.

   In what ways can you help yourself remember and believe the goodness of God's discipline and of correction by fellow believers?

   How will you think or act differently as a result of what God has revealed in His Word?

2. Pray for one another, particularly for God's help in applying the biblical truths studied and discussed during the group session.

Spend a few minutes praying for each person in the group. Ask God to reveal Himself and speak clearly to each person this week.

Prayer Requests

Encourage members to complete "This Week's Plan" before the next group session.

This Week's Plan

Work with your group leader each week to create a plan for personal study, worship, and application between group sessions. Select from the following optional activities to match your personal preferences and available time.

Worship

[ ] Read your Bible. Complete the reading plan on page 56.

[ ] Spend time with God by engaging with the devotional experience on page 57.

[ ] Connect with God every day in prayer.

Personal Study

[ ] Read and interact with "Slaves to God" on page 58.

[ ] Read and interact with "The Spotless Bride" on page 62.

Application

[ ] Memorize Matthew 18:15-20.

[ ] Identify someone in your life who can be honest with you about the sin in your life.

[ ] Connect over coffee with someone in the group. Discuss your thoughts on this week's study and your expectations for the group going forward.

[ ] Continue your journal. This week record at least five ways you can remember to fight for godliness, even when you would rather compromise in the moment.

Did you miss the group session?
Video sessions available for purchase at lifeway.com/revelation

55

Read

Read the following Scripture passages this week. Use the acronym **HEAR** and the space provided to record your thoughts or action steps.

Day 1: Revelation 2:12-29

Day 2: Romans 6

Day 3: Philippians 3

Day 4: I Corinthians 11:17-34

Day 5: 2 Corinthians 7

Day 6: I Corinthians 2

Day 7: Matthew 18:10-35

HIGHLIGHT • EXPLAIN • APPLY • RESPOND

Reflect

EXAMINING OUR HEARTS AND MINDS

I like to think I know myself better than anyone else. After all, I know what goes on in my head every second of every day—even when I'm asleep and dreaming. Since no one else can read my mind, I sometimes convince myself that people don't have the right to speak into my life.

The truth is, we're terrible judges of our own hearts. And we're good at excusing our sin, justifying our actions, and thinking we're always right. This is why Jesus cautioned the saints in Thyatira that they should heed His judgment:

> All the churches will know that I am the one who examines minds
> and hearts, and I will give to each of you according to your works.
> **Revelation 2:23**

God gives this standard reminder throughout Scripture. Here are a few examples:

> The LORD searches every
> heart and understands the
> intention of every thought.
> **1 Chronicles 28:9**

> The LORD is the tester of hearts.
> **Proverbs 17:3**

> May the words of my mouth and the
> meditation of my heart be acceptable to
> you, LORD, my rock and my Redeemer.
> **Psalm 19:14**

> I, the LORD, examine the
> mind, I test the heart to give
> to each according to his
> way, according to what
> his actions deserve.
> **Jeremiah 17:10**

Because God is a perfect, holy, righteous Judge who is good, we should turn to Him in prayer and in His Word. He alone truly knows us—even better than we know ourselves. And by His grace He surrounds us with wise brothers and sisters who can help us discern our motives and actions. May we open our hearts and minds to God and others as we seek to become more like Christ.

Personal Study 1

SLAVES TO GOD

Many of us believe the gospel and have dedicated our lives to Jesus, but we're still tempted to compromise our beliefs or morals under pressure. Some of us fall into sexual sin over and over again; others struggle with pride, greed, or anger. Sometimes we sin because we believe Christ's forgiveness gives us freedom to ignore spiritual discipline. The saints in Pergamum fell into these types of traps:

> Write to the angel of the church in Pergamum: Thus says the one who has the sharp, double-edged sword: I know where you live—where Satan's throne is. Yet you are holding on to my name and did not deny your faith in me, even in the days of Antipas, my faithful witness who was put to death among you, where Satan lives. But I have a few things against you. You have some there who hold to the teaching of Balaam, who taught Balak to place a stumbling block in front of the Israelites: to eat meat sacrificed to idols and to commit sexual immorality. In the same way, you also have those who hold to the teaching of the Nicolaitans. So repent! Otherwise, I will come to you quickly and fight against them with the sword of my mouth. Let anyone who has ears to hear listen to what the Spirit says to the churches. To the one who conquers, I will give some of the hidden manna. I will also give him a white stone, and on the stone a new name is inscribed that no one knows except the one who receives it.
> **Revelation 2:12-17**

In the previous passage, circle the places where Jesus commended the church. Underline the dangers and sins He warned against.

Last week we discussed persecution faced by the church in Smyrna. Christians all over this region of Asia Minor were experiencing persecution from the Roman Empire, so it's no surprise that Jesus mentioned it again. Just as the saints in Smyrna were encouraged to hold fast to Christ, those in Pergamum were given the same charge—and seemed to be doing a good job at it.

However, Jesus was more pointed with the church in Pergamum because it had the reputation of being a compromising church in other areas. Jesus opened His letter by reminding the believers that He held "the sharp, double-edged sword" (v. 12), a reminder that He was the righteous Judge who held full authority. Regardless of threats or earthly condemnation, only God's judgment truly mattered.

When you think of judgment, what comes to mind?

How does the fact that Jesus is the righteous Judge with full authority offer comfort and security to persecuted believers?

Jesus' mention of the sword let these believers know that even though the emperor might kill some of their brothers and sisters in Christ for their faith (such as Antipas, v. 13), He's the true Judge. Judgment from the emperor's throne paled in comparison to judgment from the throne of God. This was both an encouragement and a warning for the saints in Pergamum.

On the one hand, the saints in Pergamum weren't denying the faith, even in the midst of deadly persecution. They stood against the pressure to bow to Caesar. For them, "to live is Christ and to die is gain" (Phil. 1:21). Scripture is clear that all who hold tightly to their confession of faith will conquer even death (see Rev. 2:10).

On the other hand, the church in Pergamum was participating in false worship. They were holding on to their faith all the way to the point of death, but they were still being influenced by false doctrines. Jesus noted two of these false doctrines: the teaching of Balaam and the teaching of the Nicolaitans. Both of these false religions were similar.

In Numbers 22–24 we read the story of Balaam and Balak. Balaam told Balak that he could entice the Israelites to participate in prostitution as part of the Moabites' religious feasts. The saints in Pergamum were making the same mistake; they abused their grace and freedom in Christ by indulging in meat sacrificed to idols and by committing sexual immorality.

We met the Nicolaitans in our study of the church in Ephesus. One of their pagan practices was similar to those of Balaam. They taught that there was no need to restrain themselves in the areas of fornication and eating meat sacrificed to idols. They were turning their liberty into license to sin.

Read Romans 6:15-23. What point was Paul making about being a slave of God versus being a slave of sin?

If we're forgiven of any sin, why does it matter that we become slaves to God?

How do Paul's words in Romans 6 help explain Jesus' frustration with the church in Pergamum, even though they were diligent in the face of persecution?

In I Corinthians 11:17-34 Paul addressed a similar abuse of Christian freedom, warning the Corinthian church not to partake in the Lord's Supper in a dishonorable way. The point is simple: our bodies belong to the Lord, and our worship includes the way we use our bodies. This is why the doctrines of Balaam and the Nicolaitans were so dangerous. They were abuses not only of grace but also of their bodies, which belonged to the Lord.

Paul explained to the church in Corinth:

If we were properly judging ourselves, we would not be judged,

but when we are judged by the Lord, we are disciplined,

so that we may not be condemned with the world.

1 Corinthians 11:31-32

When God judges Christians, He does so with the intent of making us more like Christ and less like the world around us. Like a loving Father, He disciplines us to help us grow (see Heb. 12:6-7). So when Jesus said, "Repent! Otherwise, I will come to you quickly and fight against them with the sword of my mouth" (Rev. 2:16), He was telling the saints in Pergamum that He's serious about ongoing rebellion in the lives of believers.

Christians are never perfect, so do you think Jesus was being too harsh on the saints in Pergamum? Why or why not?

List a few ways you engage in ongoing rebellion against God.

Why is it important to repent of these sins and to hold fast to the teachings of Jesus?

Jesus concluded His letter by telling the saints that those who conquered would receive "hidden manna" and "a white stone" (v. 17). In other words, like the Israelites in Exodus 16, those who repented of ongoing rebellion would receive food that would sustain their spiritual lives. The white stone is an invitation to know God in a unique, personal way—a way the world doesn't know Him.

May we never compromise our walk with Christ by feasting on the rotting meat of false gods. May we instead feast on the source of eternal life. May we accept the white stone, Jesus' invitation to the final supper with the saints who have gone before us and will come after us (see Rev. 19:6-9). The God who promises to judge is the God who promises to save.

Personal Study 2

THE SPOTLESS BRIDE

Compromise and corruption are two sides of the same coin. Both are rooted in the idea that sacrificing truth and principles is the way to get ahead in life. Someone who compromises his or her beliefs also ends up having a corrupted heart. If we compromise, we're ultimately giving in to corruption.

Jesus commended the church in Thyatira for its "love, faithfulness, service, and endurance" (Rev. 2:19), but it also had a bad reputation for corruption. Like the church in Pergamum, the Thyatiran saints were participating in false worship, including eating meat sacrificed to idols and committing sexual sins. Jesus warned them:

> Write to the angel of the church in Thyatira: Thus says the Son of God, the one whose eyes are like a fiery flame and whose feet are like fine bronze: I know your works—your love, faithfulness, service, and endurance. I know that your last works are greater than the first. But I have this against you: You tolerate the woman Jezebel, who calls herself a prophetess and teaches and deceives my servants to commit sexual immorality and to eat meat sacrificed to idols. I gave her time to repent, but she does not want to repent of her sexual immorality. Look, I will throw her into a sickbed and those who commit adultery with her into great affliction. Unless they repent of her works, I will strike her children dead. Then all the churches will know that I am the one who examines minds and hearts, and I will give to each of you according to your works. I say to the rest of you in Thyatira, who do not hold this teaching, who haven't known "the so-called secrets of Satan"—as they say—I am not putting any other burden on you. Only hold on to what you have until I come. The one who conquers and who keeps my works to the end: I will give him authority over the nations—
>> and he will rule them with an iron scepter;
>> he will shatter them like pottery—

just as I have received this from my Father. I will also give
him the morning star. Let anyone who has ears to hear
listen to what the Spirit says to the churches.
Revelation 2:18-29

Why wouldn't this church's "love, faithfulness, service, and endurance" (v. 19) be enough? Why didn't Jesus stop there?

Jesus had begun addressing the church in Pergamum by saying He held a "sharp, double-edged sword" (v. 12). He was reminding them that His judgments were higher than the judgments of death inflicted on their martyred brothers and sisters. He opened His letter to Thyatira with a different reminder: "Thus says the Son of God, the one whose eyes are like a fiery flame and whose feet are like fine bronze" (v. 18).

Although the two churches were committing similar sins, Jesus addressed them in two different ways, primarily because they were located in two different cities with two different rulers. Pergamum literally faced the emperor's sword, and Thyatira was under the rule of Tyrimnas, who was affectionately called a son of the gods. He might have thought of himself as a son of the gods, but Jesus Himself is the true, authoritative Son of God, with eyes that pierce and purify (fire) and with feet that crush unrighteousness (bronze).

Jesus used each church's context to make His point, but His words transcend time and space: open rebellion against God, in any context and in any era of history, is unacceptable. These words are aimed at us just as much as they were aimed at the saints in Thyatira. He wants us to take our sin seriously and to genuinely repent of it.

Read 2 Corinthians 7:9-11. What phrases does this passage use to describe the results of grief that leads to repentance?

Why does grieving over your sins lead to repentance and life, not sorrow and death?

Jesus described a woman in the church in Thyatira, Jezebel, who claimed to be a prophetess and was influencing the men in the church to join in false worship involving food and sex. Although the woman's name may or may not have literally been Jezebel, the woman in the church in Thyatira must have reflected the heart and actions of Queen Jezebel, who had led Israel into idolatry and immorality (see 1 Kings 16–2 Kings 9). Jesus went on to describe what would happen to this woman and likewise to all those who didn't repent of their sins. God would bring judgment in such a way that all would have to acknowledge Jesus as "the one who examines minds and hearts" and who will give us what we deserve (Rev. 2:23).

Looking at these letters of Revelation, our own hearts, and the world around us, we can easily recognize that Satan has been successful for thousands of years in leading the people of God astray in these areas. Indulging in sexual sin and using liberty as a license to sin are nothing new. But Jesus calls us to fight against these impulses diligently and seriously.

Reflect on your week. In what ways have you sinned without repenting?

Record a short prayer, asking God to prepare your heart to receive His discipline and His grace.

I once served in a church where a member, after repeatedly rejecting the pleas of our leaders to repent, was asked to leave the church. This drastic step grieved our leaders. Godly discipline is meant to restore and direct sinners to Christ, not to condemn and harm them. Even though this person was excommunicated, the congregation responded not in rebellion but in repentance. Others learned the importance of discipline in the church. An unfortunate situation proved to be a beautiful, purifying moment for us.

You likely know a fellow Christian who's struggling with sin. List ways you can serve this person by pointing him or her to Christ.

Record a short prayer, asking God to soften this person's heart and prepare him or her for repentance.

God disciplines us because He loves us. He's a good Father. And Jesus warned these churches and our churches today because His mission is to prepare us to be His holy, blameless bride, without spot or wrinkle (see Eph. 5:27; Rev. 21:2). The cross of Christ frees us from compromise and corruption, as His Holy Spirit reminds us (see John 14:26).

Remember these words:

> The person without the Spirit does not receive what comes from God's Spirit, because it is foolishness to him; he is not able to understand it since it is evaluated spiritually. The spiritual person, however, can evaluate everything, and yet he himself cannot be evaluated by anyone. For
> who has known the Lord's mind,
> that he may instruct him?
> But we have the mind of Christ.
> **1 Corinthians 2:14-16**

> Let anyone who has ears to hear listen
> to what the Spirit says to the churches.
> **Revelation 2:29**

Sardis:
The Church That
Fell Asleep

There's no longer a military draft in the United States. Enough volunteers are available for the armed forces that people who don't want to enlist don't have to. They have a choice.

Christians, in contrast, are automatically enlisted in a battle when they confess Jesus as Lord. Though He has claimed victory in a cosmic battle through His substitutionary death on the cross, He's enlisting soldiers to join a battle that's already won but not yet fully celebrated.

In Revelation 3 the church in Sardis seemed to be vacillating on its obligation to fight in this battle. Jesus came to them and warned that if they didn't wake up, they would be caught sleeping when He returned to drive the nail into Satan's coffin. The punishment for staying asleep is eternal. The King's book of life, which records the names of soldiers enlisted in the battle and the confession of Jesus' victory, doesn't contain the names of those who sleep.

However, a few saints in Sardis remained alert. They were on the battlefield with weapons in hand and eyes peeled for the enemies surrounding them. As a result, these believers would have their names recorded in the book of life, and Jesus would acknowledge their faithfulness on the last day.

Those who remained alert would feast for eternity in the presence of their God and King, while others may forever be separated from His kingdom. The difference between them was a simple one. Those who conquered would stand beside the victorious Lord of all creation. Those who didn't would stand in defeat beside the evil, slain prince of the antikingdom.

Start

Welcome everyone to session 4 of *Letters of the Revelation*. Use the following content to begin your group session together.

In the previous group session we looked at several ways believers can compromise and become corrupt in our faith. We were encouraged to repent of ongoing rebellion toward God and to help others fight sin as well.

As you spent time in God's Word and prayer this week, in what ways did God show you that you were a slave to something other than Him?

Did you take any steps of faith in response to this revelation? If so, what did you do? If not, why not?

In this session we'll learn more about what it means to confess Christ as Lord and about staying alert to our tendency to fall asleep in our battle against sin. We'll see that Jesus promises victory for all those who confess His name and join in His redemptive mission. Let's watch as D. A. explores Jesus' words to the church in Sardis.

Read Revelation 3:1-6 in preparation for the video and then watch video session 4.

Watch

Jesus is saying that He alone, who is perfectly God, who is fully God, is the One who is fully Lord over the affairs of His church.

Jesus is the One who is building His church. We are called to be the church.

Jesus' resurrection from the grave allowed Him to disarm Satan, break the weapon of death, and now those who embrace Christ as Lord and Savior have life eternal because they know Jesus.

I lose my appetite for the things of God when I feast on the garbage of the world.

Starve yourself from the things of the world to develop an appetite for the things of God.

Keep the gospel, preserve its purity, and proclaim it for the glory of God.

If we conquer sleep, we will walk into the presence of our God. Jesus, our commanding officer, as we walk into glory, clothed in the righteousness of Jesus, will pronounce our name to our King, God the Father.

Discuss

Use the following statements and questions to discuss the video.

D. A. told a story about the time when his mother asked him to do chores while she was at work. Like a normal teenager, he didn't finish any of his chores, even though he tried to give an outward appearance that he had. When his mom looked under the bed, she saw the truth. Although he claimed that he had followed through on his promise, he hadn't.

Identify a time when you pretended to do a job but only halfway completed the work.

What were the ramifications of not completing the work?

Much like a parent who catches a teenager not keeping his or her word, Jesus told the saints in Sardis they had gone only halfway in their service for His kingdom, covering up their unfinished work with a false veneer. They had done just enough good works to look alive on the outside, but inside they were dead. Their works were like fruit that's disconnected from the tree. Thought at first it looks shiny and new at the store, it quickly rots on the kitchen counter.

In what ways would you say your excitement about the truths of the gospel has waned since you first confessed Jesus as Lord?

Discuss a biblical definition of *works*.

Now discuss an unhealthy view of works and how we can see the evidence of this in our own lives.

The world throws countless distractions at us that often keep us from focusing on the gospel. Money. Success. Relationships. Entertainment. Comfort. Affirmation. Social media. None of these things are sinful by themselves, but they're no different from the fruit in the garden that Satan used to tempt Adam and Eve. They exist to glorify God and give us joy, but if we let them replace God, they poison our souls. In the end they cause us to become spiritual zombies—walking but dead.

What idol has the strongest hold on your life?

Why is this idol incapable of replacing Jesus?

How can your group hold one another accountable to stay awake to the goodness of the gospel?

Jesus said some of the saints in Sardis were awake. They would join Jesus in eternity and would have their names written in the book of life. Jesus shed His blood and stained His clothes so that ours would be as white as snow: "The one who conquers will be dressed in white clothes" (v. 5). On the last day Jesus will acknowledge those who acknowledge this truth.

Conclude the group session with the prayer activity on the following page.

Pray

Conclude the group session with two actions.

1. Consider the group's responses to the truths of Scripture and pray for the Holy Spirit to work in our lives in the ways we've seen in God's Word.

   How can you help yourself remember and believe that Jesus is better than anything this world has to offer?

   How will you think or act differently as a result of what God has revealed in His Word?

2. Pray for one another, particularly for God's help in applying the biblical truths studied and discussed during the group session.

Spend a few minutes praying for each person in the group. Ask God to reveal Himself and speak clearly to each person this week.

Prayer Requests

Encourage members to complete "This Week's Plan" before the next group session.

This Week's Plan

Work with your group leader each week to create a plan for personal study, worship, and application between group sessions. Select from the following optional activities to match your personal preferences and available time.

Worship

[ ] Read your Bible. Complete the reading plan on page 74.

[ ] Spend time with God by engaging with the devotional experience on page 75.

[ ] Connect with God every day in prayer.

Personal Study

[ ] Read and interact with "Wake Up!" on page 76.

[ ] Read and interact with "Warriors Dressed in White" on page 80.

Application

[ ] Memorize Revelation 3:3-5.

[ ] Identify someone in your life who can be honest with you about the sin in your life.

[ ] Connect over coffee with someone in the group. Discuss your thoughts on this week's study and your expectations for the group going forward.

[ ] Continue your journal. This week record at least five ways you can remember to seek joy in the gospel rather than in other things.

Did you miss the group session?
Video sessions available for purchase at lifeway.com/revelation

73

Read

Read the following Scripture passages this week. Use the acronym **HEAR** and the space provided to record your thoughts or action steps.

Day 1: Revelation 3:1-6

Day 2: Matthew 16:13-28

Day 3: Romans 10

Day 4: Ephesians 2:1-10

Day 5: Hebrews 10:19-39

Day 6: 2 Chronicles 15:1-7

Day 7: Hebrews 4:14-16

Reflect

MORE THAN ZOMBIES

A recent obsession with zombies in our culture has given rise to movies, TV shows, and bands built on the idea of dead people walking. Perhaps it's the seeming impossibility of zombieness that intrigues people.

Many Christians walk around in an almost zombielike state. We stumble around, breathing but not really living. Though we're not six feet under, we're dead. Jesus warned the saints in Sardis about this very problem:

> You have a reputation for being alive, but you are dead. Be alert and strengthen what remains, which is about to die, for I have not found your works complete before my God.
> **Revelation 3:1-2**

Zombies are like walking, grumbling unfinished business. They're in limbo, between life and death. Only their actions give the appearance of life. In contrast to physical or spiritual zombies, Christians have real hope of life after death. We too will escape the grave, but we'll be truly alive. Our deaths will be real, but so will the beating hearts in our chests:

> Truly I tell you, an hour is coming, and is now here, when the dead will hear the voice of the Son of God, and those who hear will live. For just as the Father has life in himself, so also he has granted to the Son to have life in himself. And he has granted him the right to pass judgment, because he is the Son of Man. Do not be amazed at this, because a time is coming when all who are in the graves will hear his voice and come out—those who have done good things, to the resurrection of life, but those who have done wicked things, to the resurrection of condemnation.
> **John 5:25-29**

Those who have faith in Christ will be resurrected to life, unbelievers to death. The difference will be their alertness to the gospel in this life.

Personal Study 1

WAKE UP!

In the video I shared a story about my wife's lasagna. It's one of the best dishes on planet Earth, but there are still times when I don't appreciate it the way I should. This, of course, hurts my wife—and rightly so!

But how much more is God offended when we don't appreciate and submit to the gospel? When we'd rather feast on the world than feast on the gospel, we show with our actions that the gospel isn't supreme in our lives. We treat it like a take-or-leave compartment of our lives. This was the situation in which we find the church in Sardis:

> Write to the angel of the church in Sardis: Thus says the one who has the seven spirits of God and the seven stars: I know your works; you have a reputation for being alive, but you are dead. Be alert and strengthen what remains, which is about to die, for I have not found your works complete before my God. Remember, then, what you have received and heard; keep it, and repent. If you are not alert, I will come like a thief, and you have no idea at what hour I will come upon you. But you have a few people in Sardis who have not defiled their clothes, and they will walk with me in white, because they are worthy. In the same way, the one who conquers will be dressed in white clothes, and I will never erase his name from the book of life but will acknowledge his name before my Father and before his angels. Let anyone who has ears to hear listen to what the Spirit says to the churches.
> **Revelation 3:1-6**

In what ways do you tend to feast on the things of this world instead of on the truths of Scripture?

Jesus told the church in Sardis that He knew their works—works that were making them dead instead of alive in Christ. Describe the warning Jesus gave the church if they didn't wake up and strengthen their faith.

In what ways are you tempted to perform works that build your reputation? How does this self-serving effort lead toward death instead of life?

Jesus is the only One who can save us from the wrath of God that we've brought on ourselves through our sin. Since the first disobedience of Adam and Eve, sin has run rampant through the human race, causing separation from God and other people. This separation has opened the door to idolatry—the worship of false gods. And that's exactly what was going on in the church in Sardis. Instead of completing works for the kingdom of God, they were substituting things they thought would give them life for the worship of God. And tragically, those things were bringing death—not life.

In His resurrection Jesus defeated our greatest enemy—death. Death is the inevitable result of our sinful condition, and we seek eternal physical and spiritual death when we divert our worship, praise, and adulation away from God. Confessing and submitting to the lordship of the resurrected Jesus Christ, God in the flesh, is our only hope of eternal life. Idolatry leads to death; worshiping the one true God leads to life.

Read Genesis 3:1-7. In what way was the first sin an act of idolatry?

In what ways do we believe the same lie of Satan today?

Jesus opened this letter to the church in Sardis by calling Himself "the one who has the seven spirits of God and the seven stars" (Rev. 3:1). The number 7 is the number of completion, so Jesus was indicating that He alone is the full, perfect Lord over His church.

Jesus' lordship over the church is rooted in His declaration that He's building a church—a fellowship, a body, a bride—that will storm the gates of hell and destroy the counterfeit kingdom of Satan:

> When Jesus came to the region of Caesarea Philippi, he asked his disciples, "Who do people say that the Son of Man is?" They replied, "Some say John the Baptist; others, Elijah; still others, Jeremiah or one of the prophets." "But you," he asked them, "who do you say that I am?" Simon Peter answered, "You are the Messiah, the Son of the living God." Jesus responded, "Blessed are you, Simon son of Jonah, because flesh and blood did not reveal this to you, but my Father in heaven. And I also say to you that you are Peter, and on this rock I will build my church, and the gates of Hades will not overpower it. I will give you the keys of the kingdom of heaven, and whatever you bind on earth will have been bound in heaven, and whatever you loose on earth will have been loosed in heaven."
> **Matthew 16:13-19**

Peter's confession was right: Jesus is Lord. He's the Messiah and the Son of God. The church is the vehicle through which His authority would spread to the ends of the earth (see Matt. 28:18-20). Like Peter, many of those in Sardis correctly made this confession. But like Peter in his later denials of Jesus (see Luke 22:54-62), they were in danger of not following through on their confession.

Why was it so hard for Peter, the saints in Sardis, and us to hold fast to our confession of Christ every second of every day?

Why is it important that the church belongs to Jesus and not to us?

Jesus told the church in Sardis to be alert (see Rev. 3:2). In other words, "Wake up!" They had gotten lazy. We can assume that at some point they were committed to the truths of the gospel, but their senses had been dulled. They were falling asleep at the wheel, and their impaired judgment was bringing them dangerously close to flying off the road.

If you've ever been robbed or have known someone who's been a victim of robbery, it's hard to imagine a good thief. It's difficult to get excited when you hear a story about someone breaking into a home or business, stealing personal belongings, or vandalizing property. Yet oddly, Jesus referred to Himself in this passage as a thief who would come unexpectedly (see v. 3).

Obviously, Jesus wasn't a criminal. He intended this illustration to shock the saints in Sardis. He wanted to get their attention, and what better way than to unsettle their slumber with the idea that their sleep shouldn't have been as sound as it had become?

What comes to mind when you think of waking up in the middle of the night to a thief in your house?

How did Jesus use a negative illustration to make a good point?

Jesus also told the church to "strengthen what remains" (v. 2). The word *strengthen* conveys the idea of making something permanent. In other words, take a gospel Red Bull®, get your adrenaline pumping again, and refocus on what's most important. Don't fall asleep, taking your confession of Jesus to the grave with you, and don't abandon the mission He gave you.

Personal Study 2

WARRIORS DRESSED IN WHITE

Jesus is Lord. This is a statement we have to say again and again every day of our lives. Many in Sardis forgot this truth. Maybe they got lazy or bored or distracted. But one thing is for sure: they didn't stay alert. And now they were in danger of not finishing the race they had started when they first proclaimed Jesus as Lord.

Confession of faith, something the church in Sardis was likely failing at, isn't merely a personal thing for believers. It's a declaration to the world that Jesus is building His church and that the world is being reconciled to God. Christianity isn't a private secret; it's a public invitation to confess that the risen Lord Jesus is alive and is making us alive with Him.

Paul discussed this idea of confession and salvation in his letter to the Romans:

> If you confess with your mouth, "Jesus is Lord," and believe in your heart that God raised him from the dead, you will be saved. One believes with the heart, resulting in righteousness, and one confesses with the mouth, resulting in salvation. For the Scripture says, Everyone who believes on him will not be put to shame, since there is no distinction between Jew and Greek, because the same Lord of all richly blesses all who call on him. For everyone who calls on the name of the Lord will be saved.
> **Romans 10:9-13**

Why does Scripture emphasize our outward confession of faith in Christ? Why can't we simply believe privately in our hearts?

In what ways do you shy away from outwardly confessing Jesus as Lord?

Jesus noted that a few saints in Sardis had stayed alert. They hadn't fallen into a slumber and forgotten their confession of Jesus. They were still on mission, still looking to Jesus above all things. Because they hadn't "defiled their clothes," they would walk with Jesus "in white, because they are worthy" (Rev. 3:4).

Jesus pointed out these undefiled saints for a reason: they were examples to the rest of the congregation. He said in effect, "This is what you should be doing." This doesn't mean they were perfect; it means even in their imperfection they were alert and were staying focused on Christ.

> **Who in your life has been an example of keeping his or her eyes focused on Jesus, even in imperfection and struggles?**

> **Who in your life is looking to you as an example of godliness?**

> **Who in your life needs to hear your confession of Jesus as Lord?**

In ancient times when warriors came back from victory, they dressed in white togas and joined the city in a celebration of their victory. The city threw a parade, and the warriors marched through the city all the way to the palace. When they arrived at the king's banquet hall, the general of the army pronounced the names of the soldiers to the king, telling the king about the great battle they had fought.

The sleepy members of the church in Sardis would have recognized that Jesus was encouraging them with this illustration. It's equally encouraging to those of us today who nod off and fall short of confessing Christ. If we fight sleep and join the battle, we'll be presented without blemish before the King at the final banquet (see Rev. 19:6-9).

In what ways is the Christian life a battle?

How does King Jesus' promise in these verses give us cause to wake up and join the fight?

The metaphor of the Christian life as a battle is found in numerous places in Scripture. One notable reference is in Paul's letter to the Ephesians:

> Be strengthened by the Lord and by his vast strength. Put on the full armor of God so that you can stand against the schemes of the devil. For our struggle is not against flesh and blood, but against the rulers, against the authorities, against the cosmic powers of this darkness, against evil, spiritual forces in the heavens. For this reason take up the full armor of God, so that you may be able to resist in the evil day, and having prepared everything, to take your stand. Stand, therefore, with truth like a belt around your waist, righteousness like armor on your chest, and your feet sandaled with readiness for the gospel of peace. In every situation take up the shield of faith with which you can extinguish all the flaming arrows of the evil one. Take the helmet of salvation and the sword of the Spirit—which is the word of God. Pray at all times in the Spirit with every prayer and request, and stay alert with all perseverance and intercession for all the saints.
> **Ephesians 6:10-18**

Paul used not only the same battle image to describe the Christian life but also the same language of staying alert. Can you imagine a warrior who's standing on the battlefield asleep without any armor? Aside from looking a little silly, he would be of no use to his comrades. He would be a sitting duck for the enemy, and his fellow soldiers couldn't rely on him for support.

Jesus was telling the church in Sardis that if the entire army wasn't awake and ready to fight, they would be casualties in war. No victory parade to the King's palace. No chance of wearing white victory garments. The only way to have victory is to look at the King who stands in the battle ahead of them and be alert to His call to jump into the fray.

Underline each spiritual discipline listed in Ephesians 6:10-18.

List below, in order of frequency, which of these disciplines you engage in most often.

List some ways you can more intentionally practice the disciplines near the bottom of your list.

Praise God that Jesus has already secured the victory for all those who confess His name and join His mission of reconciliation in the world. The cross was a victor's chariot, carrying Him from a bloody death to the tomb from which He burst forth. The pressure isn't on us to win the war; instead, we're called to be faithful warriors in our victorious King's battle.

If we conquer sleep, we'll walk into the presence of God, clothed in Jesus' spotless, unblemished righteousness. He will confess our names to God, telling Him of the great battle in which we fought. Standing before God, we'll hear, "Well done, good and faithful servant!" (Matt. 25:21). Our names will be in His book of life, and no one will ever blot them out. The gates of hell will be crushed, and we'll spend eternity with our King.

Philadelphia: The Church That Endured

Week 5

Family reunions can be exhausting, awkward, and just plain crazy. These are the times when you see that uncle you would never want to claim in public or that great aunt who's always making inappropriate comments. Family reunions can be one big circus, but they're also beautiful.

At a family reunion we spend time with people who live both near and far away. These people are our blood. They might be a little crazy, but they're our crazy. As strange as it seems, we wouldn't have them any other way.

God the Son stepped out of eternity and into our chaos for the same reason: His family was scattered all over the place, and sin had made them eternally crazy. But they were His. Born of a virgin on what seemed like an ordinary night in Bethlehem, a baby joined a family so that He could begin His mission of reconciling that family with the Father.

In Jesus we have a Brother who loves us despite the disease that has poisoned our souls, and His death on the cross shows that He will do anything to ensure that our eternal family reunion happens as planned.

The church in Philadelphia, a small gathering of people from God's family, had remained faithful. Unlike other churches in Asia Minor, they had endured. And Jesus encouraged them to keep at it. Their perseverance was a proclamation of the gospel, and their unashamed testimony is an example to all of us. Their faithfulness to Jesus was a resounding witness to the unmatched grace of God.

Start

Welcome everyone to session 5 of *Letters of the Revelation*. Use the following content to begin your group session together.

In the previous group session we were encouraged to be alert and ready to fight for godliness. We saw that as soldiers of the King, we battle in His service.

> As you spent time in God's Word and prayer this week, in what specific ways did God show you that you were spiritually asleep and needed to wake up?

> Did you take any steps of faith in response to this revelation? If so, what did you do? If not, why not?

> List some ways you can respond to God's call to be alert to His mission in the world.

In this session we'll learn more about the uniqueness and power of Jesus' offer of salvation. We'll see that Jesus is the cornerstone of our faith, calling us to endure both in times of comfort and in times of suffering. Let's watch as D. A. tells us more about Jesus' words to the church in Philadelphia.

Read Revelation 3:7-13 in preparation for the video and then watch video session 5.

Watch

Use the space below to follow along and take notes as you watch video session 5.

Jesus is the One who holds the messianic key to open God's saving grace of redemption so that people from every nation, tribe, and tongue who call upon the name of Jesus Christ to be saved will be brought into the household of God.

Jesus is the open-door policy for God's saving grace to humanity.

Jesus left the comforts of His house, which is heaven, and came and preached peace with God for those who were enemies of God.

May we be unashamed with the gospel message, proclaiming that the human race is fallen into sin, and point all eyes to our Savior, Jesus Christ, who did everything that was necessary to save us from the due penalty for our sin.

Discuss

Use the following statements and questions to discuss the video.

D. A. described two families who came over for a visit, one close by and one far away. In both cases D. A. left the comfort of his home to find them and bring them home with him.

> **Identify a time when you were lost and someone went out of his or her way to help you.**

> **How did that single act change the course of your day?**

Read aloud Luke 19:1-10.

Zacchaeus was a wee little man, but he was more than that. He was a person seeking the Seeker. As a tax collector, Zacchaeus was scum in the eyes of his neighbors. He was a thief, not a man of generosity. Yet after he was changed by Jesus, he was willing to give away the wealth he had accumulated. He was lost, and then he was found.

> **Why do you think Zacchaeus was so willing to be generous after living a life of accumulation?**

> **What can we learn from Zacchaeus's response to Jesus?**

Jesus said He had come "to seek and to save the lost" (v. 10). Zacchaeus was the perfect example of someone who was wandering far off, needing Jesus to meet him where he was and ultimately bring him home. Like all of us at one time or another, Zacchaeus wasn't looking for Jesus, but he couldn't help being changed when he met Him.

Reflect on your salvation story. How did you first come to know Jesus?

Whether you became a Christian at a young age or later in life, how would you say your life is different after meeting Jesus?

What trials has Jesus helped you endure that you wouldn't have been able to endure without Him?

Each of the saints in Philadelphia, at some point, had met Jesus for the first time. They all had stories, just like Zacchaeus and just like you and me. And through all the trials and suffering they no doubt faced, given the time and place in which they lived, they remained faithful to Jesus. They didn't walk away from Him or make excuses for not serving Him. Instead, they pressed into the grace of God.

We can learn a lot from the perseverance of the church in Philadelphia. May we heed Jesus' words:

I am coming soon. Hold on to what you have,
so that no one takes your crown.
Revelation 3:11

Conclude the group session with the prayer activity on the following page.

Pray

Conclude the group session with two actions.

1. Consider the group's responses to the truths of Scripture and pray for the Holy Spirit to work in our lives in the ways we've seen in God's Word.

   In what ways can you help yourself remember and believe that Jesus stands as the victor of the battle against sin and death?

   How will you think or act differently as a result of what God has revealed in His Word?

2. Pray for one another, particularly for God's help in applying the biblical truths studied and discussed during the group session.

Spend a few minutes praying for each person in the group. Ask God to reveal Himself and speak clearly to each person this week.

Prayer Requests

Encourage members to complete "This Week's Plan" before the next group session.

This Week's Plan

Work with your group leader each week to create a plan for personal study, worship, and application between group sessions. Select from the following optional activities to match your personal preferences and available time.

Worship

[ ] Read your Bible. Complete the reading plan on page 92.

[ ] Spend time with God by engaging with the devotional experience on page 93.

[ ] Connect with God every day in prayer.

Personal Study

[ ] Read and interact with "The Eternal Key Holder" on page 94.

[ ] Read and interact with "Permanent Pillars in the City of God" on page 98.

Application

[ ] Memorize Revelation 3:12.

[ ] Identify someone in your life who can encourage you to persevere and can point out ways you aren't being faithful.

[ ] Connect over coffee with someone in the group. Discuss this week's study and your expectations for the group going forward.

[ ] Continue your journal. This week record at least five ways Jesus' faithfulness to you helps you remain faithful to Him.

Did you miss the group session?
Video sessions available for purchase at lifeway.com/revelation

91

Read

Read the following Scripture passages this week. Use the acronym **HEAR** and the space provided to record your thoughts or action steps.

Day 1: Revelation 3:7-13

Day 2: Romans 1:16-17

Day 3: John 6:22-59

Day 4: John 10:1-18

Day 5: Galatians 3:27-29

Day 6: John 14

Day 7: Ephesians 1:3-14

Reflect

WHEN EVERYTHING IS NEW

I've visited several large cities around the country. In every city the beauty of the skyline is slightly degraded by the number of cranes perched among the skyscrapers and sports arenas. These cranes represent construction—the future homes of more buildings.

When we look at the cranes, we know something new, fresh, and perhaps beautiful is on the horizon. The end of the Book of Revelation gives us hope for something new, fresh, and beautiful on a cosmic scale:

> I saw a new heaven and a new earth; for the first heaven and the first earth had passed away, and the sea was no more. I also saw the holy city, the new Jerusalem, coming down out of heaven from God, prepared like a bride adorned for her husband. Then the one seated on the throne said, "Look, I am making everything new." He also said, "Write, because these words are faithful and true." Then he said to me, "It is done! I am the Alpha and the Omega, the beginning and the end. I will freely give to the thirsty from the spring of the water of life. The one who conquers will inherit these things, and I will be his God, and he will be my son."
> **Revelation 21:1-2,5-7**

As we'll see in this week's study, God will make us pillars in this new city. We'll be permanent residents of a place with no more sin, chaos, pain, and death. The faithful and true Word of God promises redemption for all who confess the name of Jesus and who endure to the end.

Our world is filled with glimmers of future beauty, pointing to the day when the perfect city will arrive. May we offer people hope that they'll see that glorious day.

Personal Study 1

THE ETERNAL KEY HOLDER

Being the sole person to hold the keys to just about anything is a big deal. It means you have privileged access. It means you have the right to admit or deny admission to anyone seeking to get past the lock. In many ways, holding the only key to an important building, room, or box represents unqualified power.

Think of a time when you had unrestricted access to something no one else did. How did that privilege make you think about yourself? How did others view you as the key holder?

With the idea of unrestricted access in mind, read Jesus' letter to the church in Philadelphia:

Write to the angel of the church in Philadelphia: Thus says the Holy One, the true one, the one who has the key of David, who opens and no one will close, and who closes and no one opens: I know your works. Look, I have placed before you an open door that no one can close because you have but little power; yet you have kept my word and have not denied my name. Note this: I will make those from the synagogue of Satan, who claim to be Jews and are not, but are lying—I will make them come and bow down at your feet, and they will know that I have loved you. Because you have kept my command to endure, I will also keep you from the hour of testing that is going to come on the whole world to test those who live on the earth. I am coming soon. Hold on to what you have, so that no one takes your crown. The one who conquers I will make a pillar in the temple of my God, and he will never go out again. I will write on him the name of my God and the name of the city of my God—the new Jerusalem, which

comes down out of heaven from my God—and my new name. Let anyone who has ears to hear listen to what the Spirit says to the churches.
Revelation 3:7-13

Knowing a key holder has power, we can see how important it was for Jesus to open his letter to Philadelphia by identifying Himself as "the one who has the key of David" (v. 7). He was claiming unique authority.

Earlier Jesus had made the claim that He's "the First and the Last, and the Living One" who's "alive forever and ever" and holds "the keys of death and Hades" (1:17-18). By calling Himself "the Holy One" in this passage (3:7), Jesus was letting the church know that He's the perfect, eternal One who holds the keys to salvation. He's the rightful King who holds King David's keys, as well as God in the flesh.

> **Why is it important to know that Jesus is God and not merely a man, considering His opening claims to the saints in Philadelphia?**

> **How does this truth affect the way we view Jesus' ability to grant salvation and hand down righteous judgment?**

Jesus as the Davidic key holder is a direct reference to Isaiah 22:20-25, which revealed Eliakim as a foreshadow of the future Messiah. God had appointed Eliakim to have priestly duties that provided Israel with access to God. We now know that his life actually pointed to Jesus, the promised Messiah. Because Jesus fulfilled all messianic prophecies and proved to be the true and better Eliakim, the statement in Revelation 3:7 that He holds David's keys indicates that He alone is the steward of God's saving grace.

Jesus has the power to admit and deny admission to eternity. As He said in John 14:6, "No one comes to the Father except through me." And throughout the letters to the churches in Revelation, Jesus claimed that He alone won over sin and death. Our right to enter eternity with Him comes when we conquer in this life through faith in and obedience to Him.

> **In what ways does Jesus' claim to be the only way to God contradict our culture's view of salvation?**

> **Does Jesus' claim to exclusivity make you feel uncomfortable? Why or why not?**

> **How does the truth that Jesus is the only way to God make sharing the gospel with others both easier and more difficult?**

Jesus told the saints in Philadelphia, "I have placed before you an open door that no one can close" (Rev. 3:8). In other words, mere mortals can't overpower the all-powerful King of the universe. If Jesus is the way to God's salvation, no one can stand in His way.

The finished work of Jesus has provided sinners from every nation, tribe, and tongue the opportunity to receive saving grace (see Gal. 3:28; Rev. 7:9). The open-door policy of God the Father, offered through God the Son, Jesus Christ, is a clarion call for sinners. This policy and the power of the

One who opens the door should encourage churches today to take the message of the gospel to the ends of the earth. As Jesus told His disciples, when we take the gospel to people, He's with us (see Matt. 28:18-20).

How many times a month do you talk to unbelievers about God?
None   One to four   Five to ten   More than ten

Record the names of nonbelievers in your life who need to hear the gospel message.

List three ways you can begin to talk more often with these people about Jesus.

Lord Acton is often quoted as saying, "Absolute power corrupts absolutely."[1] We all know people in authority who have abused their power and people with privileged access who abuse that privilege. Our divine key holder doesn't abuse His power. In fact, He stepped into our sin and took our place on a cross stained with His own blood. When the Living One kicked open the door to the grave, He left it open for all who call on His name as Lord, Savior, and King.

Like the church in Philadelphia, we're called to remain faithful. May we accept this call, while calling others to accept it as well.

---

1. John Emerich Edward Dalberg Acton, letter to Bishop Mandell Creighton, *The Phrase Finder*, accessed April 3, 2017, http://www.phrases.org.uk/meanings/absolute-power-corrupts-absolutely.html.

Personal Study 2

PERMANENT PILLARS IN THE CITY OF GOD

In His message to the saints in Philadelphia, Jesus again pointed out that He's omniscient—all-knowing—and can see their works and ultimately their hearts. In the previous letters He followed up this statement with either a warning or a promise of judgment. But not for the Philadelphians.

Instead, Jesus said, "I know your works . . . ; you have kept my word and have not denied my name" (Rev. 3:8). Finally a church in Asia Minor that's doing it right! Jesus even promised they would conquer their adversaries because they had remained faithful to Him. He wasn't saying they had sinless perfection; only Jesus has that. He was saying they had a posture of obedience toward Him. These saints may have tripped and stumbled, but they didn't participate in ongoing rebellion like some of the other churches we've seen.

> **If Jesus were standing in front of you saying, "I know your works," what might follow that statement?**

> **No matter how you answered, why is Jesus' open-door policy good news for you?**

Jesus commended the church in Philadelphia in two specific ways.

1. Jesus told them they had "kept my word." This is a strong reference to the Philadelphia church's confession of faith. They had kept the word of Christ—the salvation message—and weren't private about it. We know this because they had apparently agitated the community of Jews, who had tried to silence them by claiming to be the true religion in town (see v. 9).

2. Jesus commended the Philadelphians because they hadn't "denied my name." They were unashamed of the name of Jesus Christ. As we see in the persecution of the saints throughout the Book of Acts, the name of Jesus is an offense to unbelievers. Paul wrote in I Corinthians 1:18-23 that the cross is a stumbling block to the lost.

Proclaiming the name of Jesus as God's exclusive means of salvation forces us to realize that salvation is a gift of grace, not something we can earn or deserve. To an unbelieving world that looks inwardly or horizontally for salvation, vertically directed salvation is the pinnacle of offense. Jesus tells us not to look inwardly or at others for salvation but to lift our eyes to Him.

Read Matthew 10:32-33. We saw a similar idea in the letter to Sardis (see Rev. 3:5). Why would Jesus deny us if we deny Him?

Why can't we look inwardly or at others for salvation? Why do we tend to do this even if we know Jesus is the only way to salvation?

At first the call to crucify ourselves sounds horrible and imprisoning. Why is it the most freeing, beautiful call we could receive?

In Revelation 3:9 Jesus called the church's Jewish persecutors "the synagogue of Satan." During the first century when the church was still in its infancy, the greatest religious tension was between Jews who still practiced Judaism and Christians—both those who were Jewish Christians and non-Jewish, Gentile Christians. Jewish Christians were seen as selling out to a false religion, and Gentile Christians were seen as outsiders who were trying to join a club they weren't welcome to join.

In addressing that tension, Jesus reminded the Christians in Philadelphia that although those who were ethnically Jewish were cutting off and persecuting Christians, He alone possessed the authority to say who's in His kingdom and who's out. Remember, He holds the key to salvation's door.

These Jews received a harsh word from Jesus, who alluded to Old Testament teachings about Gentiles coming and bowing before the feet of the Jews during the messianic age (see Isa. 45:23; 49:23; 60:14; Zech. 8:20-23). Jesus reversed the teaching by saying it would be the ethnically Jewish people who would bow down at the feet of Christians (see Rev. 3:9), regardless of their ethnic identity.

What similar religious tension do we see in our culture today?

Based on His words to the Philadelphians, how does Jesus call us to respond to this religious tension?

Why can believers be confident that we'll be victorious, regardless of how the culture responds to our faith?

Christians will conquer because Jesus Himself conquered. He continually reminded the saints in Philadelphia and the other churches in Asia Minor to be faithful to Him because He had been faithful to them.

Jesus told the church in Philadelphia that He would make them "a pillar in the temple of my God" (v. 12). This image describes a place of permanence in God's kingdom. The pillar of the temple was a permanent fixture in the construction of the building (see 1 Kings 7:21; Jer. 1:18; Gal. 2:9).

Jesus comforted the church by making them aware that their invitation to walk through God's open door, receiving His saving grace, made them permanently secure as the people of God (see Rev. 22:4). Writing on us the name of God's city (see 3:12) shows ownership. Through Jesus' shed blood we've been ransomed and redeemed (see Eph. 1:7), and we're His possession (see 1 Pet. 2:9).

Record a few ways being owned by God changes the way you look at suffering, pressure, or tension in your life.

Read Ephesians 1:13-14. How does the Holy Spirit play a role in making us permanently belong to God?

Jesus' words should comfort us, no matter what persecution or tribulation we're facing. If we've embraced Jesus as Savior, we have right standing before God as recipients of grace. As His children, we're protected.

The truths Jesus conveyed to the church in Philadelphia should motivate us to unashamedly share the gospel of Jesus Christ. We should mirror the church's faithfulness to the word of Christ, all the while refusing to deny His name. As residents of the new Jerusalem (see Rev. 3:12; 21–22), we've already been stamped with the name of God's eternal city and with the name of the One who holds the key to that city in His hand.

Laodicea:
The Church That
Turned Lukewarm

Week 6

In any team activity—whether in sports, business, classwork, or family—people must figure out how to work together. If one person goes rogue, he or she can harm everyone on the team. In worst-case scenarios one person who strays from the mission can destroy the entire project.

Christianity isn't a solo religion. Nor is it an American or African or Asian religion. It's a vibrant community of people from around the globe, made up of every tribe, language, and nation. We're Jesus' body, and He's our Head (see Col. 1:18).

The churches throughout Asia Minor, the subjects of these letters in the Book of Revelation, are always addressed as a church body, not merely as individual people. The Greek word for *church* is *ekklesia*, meaning "the gathering" or "the gathered ones." The church isn't a person. It's a people who fix their eyes on the person of Christ.

In this final letter Jesus called the church in Laodicea to put away their lukewarm ways before He vomited them out of His mouth. They were collectively a lukewarm church, apathetic and half-hearted in faith, materially rich but spiritually poor. They were full of everything except red-hot faith in Jesus.

Jesus told the church to band together and buy riches from Him that would last and healing that only He could give. In His warning He showed His loving patience. He was standing at the door and knocking, giving this church an opportunity to repent and open the door to Him. If they did, they would be able to join His eternal kingdom—both in this life and in the life to come.

Start

Welcome everyone to session 6 of *Letters of the Revelation*. Use the following content to begin your group session together.

In the previous group session we were encouraged to hold on to the promise of God's salvation in the midst of suffering or persecution. We looked at Jesus' promise to secure our salvation and the imperative of sharing this good news with others.

> **As you spent time in God's Word and prayer this week, in what ways did God show you that your salvation is secure in Christ alone?**
>
> **Did you take any steps of faith in response to this revelation? If so, what did you do? If not, why not?**

In this session we'll learn what it means to become lukewarm in our faith. Jesus' words will challenge us to realize our need for Him. Let's watch as D. A. tells us more about Jesus' words to the church in Laodicea.

Read Revelation 3:14-22 in preparation for the video and then watch video session 6.

Watch

Spiritual bankruptcy says, "Spiritually, I was born dead in sin. Spiritually, I'm a slave to sin. Spiritually, there was a debt from my sin hanging over my head, and I can make no contribution to paying off my debt."

We must come to the point where we declare spiritual bankruptcy. We acknowledge, "I'm in debt. I can't pay off my debt. Jesus, save me from the penalty of my debt," and His blood washes it away.

The gospel reminds us of the depth of the love that the Father has for us.

When we heard the gospel, and the Holy Spirit quickened our heart to embrace Jesus Christ, we were adopted into the family of God, so now we are His children; we are coheirs with Jesus Christ.

One of the greatest stumbling blocks that prevent us from this level of humility is pride.

The greatest way that we can walk in victory over being lukewarm is by having humility as the rhythm of our lives.

We can stay on fire for God if we just stay humble and broken before Him.

Discuss

D. A. described his love for coffee, stating that he likes it piping hot. Most of us know that lukewarm coffee isn't great. Lukewarmness is the perfect temperature of mediocrity.

Jesus described the church in Laodicea as lukewarm. On the one hand, they weren't ice cold, denying Jesus' name. But on the other hand, they weren't on fire for Jesus' name and fame either.

> In what ways have you been lukewarm in your faith?
>
> How did you recognize your lukewarmness? How did you overcome it, or how are you currently working to overcome it?
>
> Reread Revelation 3:17. What emotions or convictions does this verse stir in you?

Read aloud Matthew 7:13-23.

> What did Jesus mean by "the narrow gate" (v. 13)? Why wouldn't the gate to salvation be wide open for every person to walk through?
>
> What did Jesus say about faith and works?

The passage from Matthew 7 points out that we can do all sorts of good works in Jesus' name, but we have to know Him—or rather be "known by God" (Gal. 4:9)—in order to be saved. It's one thing to know about Jesus, but it's another thing to have a deep relationship with Him that's built on complete dependence. Works in Jesus' name that aren't done from intense love for Him aren't really done in His name at all.

D. A. said in the same way, the church in Laodicea became lukewarm because they got too comfortable. By the world's standards they were rich and felt they had everything they needed. As a result, they weren't as dependent on Jesus as they should have been.

> **Reread Revelation 3:20. What's your immediate reaction to this verse after reading the harsh words that precede it?**

> **According to the video, what does it mean for Jesus to be able to perfectly assess our hearts?**

> **Why is it important not only to do good works in Jesus' name but also to do them from love for Him?**

The saints in Laodicea seemed to have been doing good works in Jesus' name but without much passion. It's not that they were doing nothing; it's that they were in limbo between nothing and gospel-fueled passion for Jesus.

> **How does our inability to earn our salvation affect the way we serve God and others?**

> **What can we learn from those to whom Jesus said, "I never knew you" (Matt. 7:23)?**

Because of Jesus' shed blood, we're not required to serve God from duty or from an effort to earn access to heaven. Instead, we're free to serve Him and others from love and gratitude. Grace elicits gratefulness.

People without shackles can dance about their freedom. And when people see them dance, they're not interested in putting shackles on themselves. May we let people see our passion for Jesus because of the freedom He has given us.

Conclude the group session with the prayer activity on the following page.

Pray

1. Consider the group's responses to the truths of Scripture and pray for the Holy Spirit to work in our lives in the ways we've seen in God's Word.

   In what ways can you begin reigniting your fire for Jesus?

   How will you think or act differently as a result of what God has revealed in His Word?

2. Pray for one another, particularly for God's help in applying the biblical truths studied and discussed during the group session.

Spend a few minutes praying for each person in the group. Ask God to reveal Himself and speak clearly to each person this week.

Prayer Requests

Encourage members to complete "This Week's Plan" before the next group session.

This Week's Plan

Work with your group leader each week to create a plan for personal study, worship, and application between group sessions. Select from the following optional activities to match your personal preferences and available time.

Worship

[ ] Read your Bible. Complete the reading plan on page 110.

[ ] Spend time with God by engaging with the devotional experience on page 111.

[ ] Connect with God every day in prayer.

Personal Study

[ ] Read and interact with "Gaining the World and Losing Our Lives" on page 112.

[ ] Read and interact with "Perfect Discipline" on page 116.

Application

[ ] Memorize Revelation 3:20-21.

[ ] Identify someone in your life who can help you recognize your need to be dependent on Jesus.

[ ] Connect over coffee with someone in the group. Discuss this week's study and your expectations for the group going forward.

[ ] Continue your journal. This week record at least five reasons lukewarm faith isn't what God calls you to.

Did you miss the group session?
Video sessions available for purchase at lifeway.com/revelation

109

Read

Read the following Scripture passages this week. Use the acronym HEAR and the space provided to record your thoughts or action steps.

Day 1: Revelation 3:14-22

Day 2: Isaiah 65:13-25

Day 3: Matthew 19:16-30

Day 4: Romans 8:31-39

Day 5: Romans 12

Day 6: 2 Peter 3

Day 7: John 16:25-33

Reflect

A HISTORY OF RECONCILIATION

God loves His people. His grace was evident from the moment He created humankind. He placed them in a garden that flourished with abundance and beauty and gave them dominion over all He had created. In a sense God made us kings and queens of this world, under His eternal kingship:

> God blessed them, and God said to them, "Be fruitful, multiply,
> fill the earth, and subdue it. Rule the fish of the sea, the birds
> of the sky, and every creature that crawls on the earth."
> **Genesis 1:28**

Though Adam and Eve sinned, God showed them immediate grace and love. Like a good Father, He went and found His lost, cowering children. He disciplined them, but He also protected them:

> The LORD God made clothing from skins for
> the man and his wife, and he clothed them.
> **Genesis 3:21**

Although the couple's sin brought shame (see 3:8-10), God covered their nakedness. Sin took them out of the garden and fractured their relationship with God, but He didn't abandon them.

Again and again in Scripture we see God moving His people toward redemption. Through the story of Adam and Eve, the law, the wisdom literature, the prophets, the ministry of Jesus, the establishment of the church, and even here in Jesus' words to the church of Laodicea, God's mission of reconciling all things to Himself is on full display. God's loving patience with us, though we disobey and curse Him time and time again, is shown in the grace He gives us to endure all the way to sinless, uninterrupted eternity with Him.

Personal Study 1

GAINING THE WORLD AND LOSING OUR LIVES

Some people are good at taking tests. Others are terrible at it. Jesus assessed the church in Laodicea and found them lacking. They were like students who aren't total failures but aren't acing the exam either. Let's look at Jesus' words to learn how these saints were falling short:

> Write to the angel of the church in Laodicea: Thus says the Amen, the faithful and true witness, the originator of God's creation: I know your works, that you are neither cold nor hot. I wish that you were cold or hot. So, because you are lukewarm, and neither hot nor cold, I am going to vomit you out of my mouth. For you say, "I'm rich; I have become wealthy and need nothing," and you don't realize that you are wretched, pitiful, poor, blind, and naked. I advise you to buy from me gold refined in the fire so that you may be rich, white clothes so that you may be dressed and your shameful nakedness not be exposed, and ointment to spread on your eyes so that you may see. As many as I love, I rebuke and discipline. So be zealous and repent. See! I stand at the door and knock. If anyone hears my voice and opens the door, I will come in to him and eat with him, and he with me. To the one who conquers I will give the right to sit with me on my throne, just as I also conquered and sat down with my Father on his throne. Let anyone who has ears to hear listen to what the Spirit says to the churches.
> **Revelation 3:14-22**

Jesus always had a reason for introducing Himself as He did to the seven churches. Jesus referred to Himself as the Amen in verse 14 because He was about to share His assessment of the church in Laodicea. He was speaking to them in real time about their present actions, pointing out that they had a higher view of themselves than God did. Because Jesus was the Amen, His pronouncement would come to be.

Jesus also called Himself "the faithful and true witness" (v. 14). This title indicated that the testimony He was about to give was completely accurate. His grading of the congregation's work was without fault because Jesus embodies capital-T Truth.

Finally, Jesus called Himself "the originator of God's creation" (v. 14). This title is similar to the one in Revelation 1:5: "the firstborn from the dead." We must couple this designation with the understanding that Jesus is the Creator, not a created being (see John 1:3) and that everything was created by Him, through Him, and for Him (see Col. 1:16). Scripture teaches that Jesus wasn't created but is rather the Creator (as God) and the blueprint for a perfect new creation (as a sinless man).

Together these names indicate that as God in the flesh who lived a perfect life, Jesus is able to truly separate lukewarm faith from true, committed faith. As we've seen many times, He's able to judge our hearts, and His judgment is always right.

> **How can we know Jesus' assessment is 100 percent right? Why is it important for Jesus' assessment to be 100 percent right?**

Jesus began His assessment by telling the church in Laodicea that they were neither cold nor hot but rather in the middle—lukewarm. While Jesus was "the faithful and true witness" (Rev. 3:14), their faith was wavering and questionable.

The saints in Laodicea would have interpreted the term *lukewarm* based on their cultural context. The nearby city of Colossae had cold, refreshing water. On the other side of their city was the town of Hierapolis, which was known for its hot springs. And because Laodicea sat between these two cities, the water that ran through it was lukewarm.

As you can imagine, lukewarm water isn't ideal for drinking or bathing. Colossae had cold water to refresh the people on hot days. Hierapolis had hot water, which is great for bathing and purifying items. Lukewarm water, like lukewarm coffee, is good only for unsettling your stomach. Jesus told the Laodiceans that like their lukewarm water, their lukewarm faith was sterile and useless.

How would you rate your spiritual temperature on the scale?

0	I	2	3	4	5	6	7	8	9	10
Ice cold				Lukewarm					Piping hot	

List a few moments or areas of your life that have caused you to become less than piping hot in your passion for God.

Jesus told the saints in Laodicea that their wealth and possessions were the reasons for their lukewarm faith. Because of financial success and an abundance of material goods, the church assumed they were in good standing with God. As a result, they grew comfortable and complacent.

But Jesus didn't let the church get away with a complacent attitude. He set the record straight, telling the Laodiceans they were "wretched, pitiful, poor, blind, and naked" (Rev. 3:17). Remember, Jesus' assessment is completely accurate. Whether or not they liked it, Jesus was right because He's faithful and true. And at that moment they weren't measuring up. They were going through life lackadaisically, and they thought they didn't need Jesus as much as they once did: "You say, 'I'm rich; I have become wealthy and need nothing' " (v. 17), Jesus stated.

Do you tend to be entirely dependent on Jesus or entirely dependent on yourself? Why do you think you trend in that direction?

Why is it disastrous to rely on yourself or someone else for salvation or even for your basic needs in life?

In what ways can you fight the temptation to rely on yourself?

Believers shouldn't be lulled to sleep by success. We shouldn't measure our lives by our wealth. Even churches shouldn't be measured by the size of their budgets, buildings, or congregations. All success, both personal and congregational, should be measured by the effectiveness of consistent love for God, disciple making, preaching of the gospel, compassionate ministry, and total reliance on Jesus for everything we have and need.

Jesus tells us here to buy what we need from Him:

> I advise you to buy from me gold refined in the fire so that you may be rich,
> white clothes so that you may be dressed and your shameful nakedness
> not be exposed, and ointment to spread on your eyes so that you may see.
> **Revelation 3:18**

Jesus has purchased on the cross all that's good, right, and necessary for us to have abundant, fruitful life in Him. As He taught His disciples:

> What will it benefit someone if he gains the whole world yet loses
> his life? Or what will anyone give in exchange for his life?
> **Matthew 16:26**

Personal Study 2

PERFECT DISCIPLINE

As we've seen elsewhere in this study, godly discipline is a good thing, even when it doesn't feel like it at the moment. As a father, I know this is true. As imperfect as I am at rightly motivated discipline, my goal in disciplining my kids isn't merely behavior modification; it's heart transformation.

Give examples of good and bad disciplinary techniques.

What criteria do you use to decide what discipline is good or bad?

God doesn't discipline from uncontrolled anger or without reason. He disciplines from love. We see this fact throughout Scripture, and Jesus made it clear to the church in Laodicea: "As many as I love, I rebuke and discipline" (Rev. 3:19). God's loving purpose is to make us more like Jesus and to renew our minds from the corruption of sin (see Rom. 8:29; 12:2).

It's sometimes considered taboo today to talk about God's hating sin and being wrathful toward sinfulness (see Ps. 5:4; Deut. 12:31; Rom. 1:18). One reason we're uncomfortable with this idea is that we've never seen hate or wrath that's perfect. All human anger, hatred, and wrath are rooted in and flow from sin. God's anger doesn't. It's rooted in love and righteousness. Because He's perfect and sinless, His discipline is also perfect and sinless.

You see, God is reconciling the world to Himself. He's unbreaking all that's broken. He's making all things new. Sin has caused a disruption in the goodness of God's creation, and He's determined to eradicate the world of sin, evil, pain, and death (see Rev. 19–22). This good purpose will be accomplished through the wrath of the perfect, sovereign God who loves us.

Does the idea that God could hate something or be wrathful make you feel uncomfortable? Why or why not?

Why is God's perfect, sinless wrath toward sin good news for us?

Jesus' discipline in Revelation 3:19 isn't fire from the heavens or another flood. Rather, His discipline echoes the words of Peter: "The Lord ... is patient with you, not wanting any to perish but all to come to repentance" (2 Pet. 3:9). Jesus showed His patience and desire for the Laodiceans' repentance by giving them advance warning of discipline. Jesus also showed the Laodiceans the eternal reward for opening up their hearts to Him:

> See! I stand at the door and knock. If anyone hears my voice and opens the door, I will come in to him and eat with him, and he with me. To the one who conquers I will give the right to sit with me on my throne, just as I also conquered and sat down with my Father on his throne.
> **Revelation 3:20-21**

Jesus wasn't kicking the door in. He was standing outside and knocking, calling the whole church to fix their collective eyes on Him and repent. He was graciously inviting them to escape wrath and obtain the final reward for faithfulness.

In the previous verses underline words indicating Jesus' kindness and patience.

In what ways have you seen Jesus show you the same kindness and patience He showed the Laodicean church?

"To the one who conquers" (v. 21) is a recurring phrase in Jesus' letters to the churches in Asia Minor. Regardless of the type of warning they received, Jesus always exhorted them to conquer or to find victory in Him. It's key to remember, however, that they couldn't conquer alone. They could conquer only through faith in and obedience to Jesus.

The lukewarm, wealthy saints in Laodicea weren't conquering anything with their riches. They couldn't buy grace from Jesus. They couldn't earn their way to salvation by donating money for a new church building. They couldn't trade in a few dollars for a few ounces of forgiveness. Their wealth was so inadequate that Jesus still called them poor (see v. 17). Material wealth doesn't equal spiritual riches.

Notice the way Jesus explained this truth elsewhere, after an encounter with a rich young man:

> Jesus said to his disciples, "Truly I tell you, it will be hard
> for a rich person to enter the kingdom of heaven. Again I tell
> you, it is easier for a camel to go through the eye of a needle
> than for a rich person to enter the kingdom of God."
> **Matthew 19:23-24**

Jesus made it plain: He's not impressed by our possessions. Why would He be? They're all His anyway. He's the sovereign King of the universe. He lacks nothing.

Jesus made a stark claim: it's hard for a rich person to experience eternity with God. What does this mean for believers in America, one of the wealthiest countries in the world?

In what ways do Jesus' words challenge the way you view your time, money, and other possessions?

Jesus confronted the Laodiceans' self-sufficiency: "You say, 'I'm rich; I have become wealthy and need nothing,' and you don't realize that you are wretched, pitiful, poor, blind, and naked" (Rev. 3:17). In what ways do you communicate to God that you don't need Him?

Do you think of yourself as spiritually wretched, pitiful, poor, blind, and naked? How does that affect your attitude toward God?

Jesus, the faithful and true witness, is calling every one of us to answer the door when He knocks. None of us are perfect in our walk with Christ. In one way or another, we're all lukewarm Laodiceans who need to repent and turn our eyes back to Jesus.

By the grace of God, we don't have to be perfect. Jesus was perfect for us (see Heb. 4:15). However, He calls us to repent, to turn away from our sin, and to trust in His righteousness to save us from ourselves. Though our sin runs deep, His grace runs deeper.

God doesn't want our good intentions or our sugarcoated works. He wants a full transformation of all we are. We must never settle for lukewarm faith but rather pray that God will ignite a fire in our hearts that continually burns more brightly for Him.

Leader Guide

Opening and Closing Group Sessions

Always try to engage each person at the beginning of the group session. Once a person speaks, even if only to answer a generic question, he or she is more likely to speak up later about more personal matters.

You may want to begin each session by reviewing the previous week's personal study. This review provides context for the next session and opportunities to share relevant experiences, application, or truths learned between sessions. Then set up the theme of the session's group study to prepare personal expectations.

Always open and close the session with prayer, recognizing that only the Holy Spirit brings understanding and transformation in our lives. The prayer suggestions provided in each session help members focus on Scripture, key truths, and personal application from the week's teaching.

Remember that your goal isn't just meaningful discussion but discipleship.

SESSION 1

Ephesus: The Church without Love

The questions in the "Start" section engage people in a fun conversation to get them talking and to help them begin thinking about personal identity.

Tell the group where you work and why you chose to work there.

Do you love what you do? Why or why not?

This opening series of questions provides an opportunity for the leader to be honest and to demonstrate authenticity. Your relationship with God isn't perfect. Your life isn't perfect. Talk about ways you're continuing to learn joy in all circumstances. This way you encourage others to share honestly.

Some people in the group may not be believers yet. Be sure to make them feel welcome. Let them know the group is a safe place for them to be open and honest. Remember that everybody has a story, whether or not he or she is a follower of Jesus. Allow freedom to share stories, ask questions, and admit frustrations as the study progresses.

Read aloud Revelation 1:1-3.

Always keep God's Word central during the group discussion to prevent people from getting off track and veering into speculation or opinion. Even though D. A. teaches on the video, the goal is for people to walk away knowing what the Bible says, not just what a pastor or group leader says. Asking group members to read aloud also invites greater participation and encourages their confidence as they lead in that moment.

In what ways have the words of Scripture recently taught you something about God? What did you learn?

How has reading God's Word helped you learn more about yourself?

This begins a series of questions that help group members examine their lives in light of Scripture and make personal application.

How do the acts of remembering and repenting help us keep our love for Jesus alive?

Why is it important not only to say we once loved and believed in Jesus but also to continually keep that love kindled?

What are your hopes or expectations for this study of the seven letters of Revelation?

This question is simple but important in three ways: (1) It provides clues about where people are in their spiritual journeys. (2) It helps people evaluate their spiritual lives and be intentional about their growth. (3) It provides encouragement and accountability when members know that nobody is perfect and everyone has room to grow.

Session 1 closes with a time for members to pray for one another, especially about the hopes they shared for the next six weeks.

SESSION 2

Smyrna: The Church That Was Persecuted

Start by reviewing the previous session and what you read, studied, or journaled during the week. This week's personal study may have been the first time some people in the group have consistently read portions of the Bible. Point out the importance of Scripture as the Word of God and the fact that it's best understood in context. Understanding the context of what we discuss helps prevent us from creating our own opinions about God and the Bible instead of letting the Bible shape our understanding of God.

Make the transition from the video teaching to discussion with the short summary statement provided in the group session. Don't reteach the lesson. Keep your transition minimal, using the provided sentence as your guide. This is true for any of the statements provided between questions. Feel free to say as much or as little as needed in the group, but remember that your intent is to facilitate discussion, not reteach.

Why is it important to understand that Jesus wasn't merely a man but God in the flesh?

Point out the encouraging reality that because Jesus is God, we know He lives for eternity, is perfect and in control, and judges hearts justly. Like all of us, in our own ways, the church in Smyrna was hurting. And like us, they surely struggled with trusting God in these times. But Jesus encouraged them to endure because He had already endured for them.

Identify a time in your life when you were slandered or attacked.

How did you respond to God? Were you quick to praise Him for your suffering, did you try to fix it on your own, or did you get angry at God?

Be sure this doesn't become a gripe session. The intent is to focus attention on our own lives. It's easy to affirm that others' opinions or attacks don't define us. It's more difficult to trust God's sovereignty in the midst of the pain and even forgive the offender.

Why does Jesus' story offer a better hope than Smyrna's story?

In what ways have you believed the lies of a false resurrection story instead of trusting in Jesus' resurrection?

By reflecting on these questions, group members will be challenged to think about the lie that something other than Jesus can save them.

This is a great opportunity for a gospel presentation. Don't assume everyone in the group is saved. Take advantage of this time to share your testimony of finding true life in Jesus.

SESSION 3

Pergamum and Thyatira: The Churches with Bad Reputations

Start by reviewing the previous group session and asking group members to share any insights or experiences related to the previous week's study. This step is important, so allow enough time to share and review, but be careful to protect the time needed to watch and discuss this week's video.

What are some areas of compromise and corruption you see in your life?

Why is it crucial to identify sin in our lives and churches?

How does Jesus ultimately give us victory over compromise and corruption?

Discourage group members from either putting themselves down or shifting blame to other people. The intent is to focus on our sins of compromise and corruption while ultimately looking to the cross and resurrection as our only hope for salvation. Sin is destructive, but Jesus destroyed sin.

Read aloud Matthew 18:15-20.

This passage represents a hallmark teaching on how to deal with conflict in the church. Just as important, group members should notice the communal aspect of this passage. Jesus isn't calling us to conflict-free, lonely lives but to lives that will inevitably lead to conflict with others. However, that conflict isn't irreparable.

Why is it easy to notice sins in others' lives but not in our own hearts?

What are the greatest reasons we hesitate to repent of our own sins?

What are the greatest reasons we hesitate to confront others' sins?

These questions encourage group members to think about conflict in a healthy way—the way Jesus presented in the Matthew passage. Sin isn't partial to anyone; we're all participants in its destructive ways. Yet we're called to love one another by pointing to Jesus.

Why does Jesus encourage us to bring along witnesses when we confront another believer's sin?

Why is Jesus' promise to be among us at those times so important?

Because Jesus is always among us, His grace, mercy, and forgiveness are with us as well. Confronting sin isn't an occasion for insults or condemnation but a time for brothers and sisters in Christ to lock arms and fight sin together, ultimately encouraging one another to be more like Jesus.

What can we learn about forgiveness from God's sending of Jesus to earth and from Jesus' death on the cross?

How can your group create and build a culture of discipline that's rooted in the gospel?

God could have easily left us in our sin, rebellion, and condemnation. As the righteous and perfect Judge, He had that right, but instead, He sent His only Son to die on the cross for us. Jesus' sacrifice is the greatest act of forgiveness the world will ever see. It serves as a powerful reminder that we can forgive and reconcile with anyone who sins against God or us.

Before concluding with prayer, end the group discussion with a story about a time when you experienced forgiveness from someone else. Hopefully, your honesty will encourage others to share stories and will help them see the beauty of godly confrontation and discipline.

SESSION 4
Sardis: The Church That Fell Asleep

Before the group arrives, reflect on the previous three weeks of study—both what you've learned and what you've experienced as a result. Be ready to start the session by openly sharing about your own walk with Jesus thus far in the study. Help group members consider progress toward the benefits they said they hoped to gain from the study. This reflection helps ensure that people are keeping the whole study in context while also applying what they've learned. It's a great opportunity for you, as the leader, to gauge members' growth in spiritual maturity.

Identify a time when you pretended to do a job but only halfway completed the work.

What were the ramifications of not completing the work?

These opening questions are designed to encourage the group to think about perseverance in everyday life. Jesus told the church in Sardis that they were like warriors fighting a battle they needed to complete. Their completion of the good works they started would be the ultimate proof of their faithfulness to Jesus.

In what ways would you say your excitement about the truths of the gospel has waned since you first confessed Jesus as Lord?

This is a great opportunity to share some of your own struggles in the area of perseverance. Pastors and leaders aren't immune to struggles to keep their fire for the gospel. Your continued honesty throughout the sessions enables you to engage with the study and encourages group members to be honest.

Jesus said again and again that the churches in Asia Minor should persevere to the end, conquering in this life and entering eternity through Christ's victory. Endurance doesn't mean that we work harder to be godlier but that we trust in Jesus as our Lord and Savior, knowing He's worthy of our faithfulness because of His faithfulness to us.

What idol has the strongest hold on your life?

This question helps group members look inward and find the deeper reason they're not wholly devoted to Jesus. Misplaced worship is the most foundational reason we struggle to give our entire lives to Jesus. We often idolize a relationship, success, or something else that causes us to turn our eyes away from the prize—God Himself.

We won't worship perfectly this side of eternity. Without Jesus we would work and work like the Pharisees but never get anywhere. That's why Jesus died to save us and to give us freedom in Him. Because of His love for us, we're free to pursue Him and His call on our lives.

SESSION 5

Philadelphia: The Church That Endured

Start by reviewing the previous group session and asking group members to share any insights or experiences related to the previous week's study. This step is important, so allow enough time to share and review, but be careful to protect the time needed to watch and discuss this week's video.

Identify a time when you were lost and someone went out of his or her way to help you.

How did that single act change the course of your day?

Read aloud Luke 19:1-10.

D. A. told a story about helping friends find his house. The account of Zacchaeus in the Gospel of Luke is a clear example of Jesus' serving someone who didn't deserve being served by worldly standards.

We sometimes underestimate the impact of small, seemingly inconsequential acts of kindness, but service was at the core of Jesus' ministry. The cross and resurrection were heroic, universe-altering events that were exclusive to the life of Jesus, but they were preceded by acts anyone can do—loving the lowly, serving those who are ignored, and showing grace to those who seem to be bad people.

Why do you think Zacchaeus was so willing to be generous after living a life of accumulation?

What can we learn from Zacchaeus's response to Jesus?

Jesus' kindness cut to Zacchaeus's heart. As a tax collector, he was maligned and rejected by people. He likely didn't receive much grace from others. Like Zacchaeus, we should see Jesus' unmerited grace as a transformative act in our hearts.

Reflect on your salvation story. How did you first come to know Jesus?

This series of questions is designed to encourage group members to reflect on ways Jesus has worked in their lives. It's easy in the hustle and bustle of life to forget to thank God for saving us. Use this time to share your own salvation story.

Additionally, this is an opportunity for members who may not be believers to hear stories about God's grace. More than just an information dump, studying the Bible with a group is a great way for nonbelievers to see lives that have been changed by the gospel. Encourage people to share stories with real examples of change, not just phrases like "I'm a nicer person now."

Finally, remind the group that everyone has a story and that every story is a part of God's bigger story of redeeming all things. As Jesus told the church in Philadelphia, we should keep our eyes on Him as the only One who can redeem us. Salvation is found in no other name (see Acts 4:12).

SESSION 6

Laodicea: The Church That Turned Lukewarm

Start by reviewing the previous group session and by asking group members to share any insights or experiences related to the previous week's study. This step is important, so allow enough time to share and review, but be careful to protect the time needed to watch and discuss this week's video.

In what ways have you been lukewarm in your faith?

How did you recognize your lukewarmness? How did you overcome it, or how are you currently working to overcome it?

Because this is the final week of study, it's important to highlight the big picture: Jesus conquered sin and death, and we have victory in Him. Christians can be lukewarm from time to time because we're all sinful and we all need God's grace every day. However, being lukewarm can't be the regular, long-term rhythm of our Christian lives. Help the group see that on the one hand, we're called to faithfulness and consistent worship of Jesus, but on the other hand, we're forgiven and free in the finished work of Jesus.

The group time shouldn't be used to add to group members' struggles but to encourage them to keep pressing into God's grace. Let them know the group is there to support them and pray with them as they pursue Christ.

Read aloud Matthew 7:13-23. What did Jesus mean by "the narrow gate" (v. 13)? Why wouldn't the gate to salvation be wide open for every person to walk through?

What did Jesus say about faith and works?

The point of this passage is to shock lukewarm believers, so we shouldn't try to tame Jesus' words. He's not interested in people who do good works without trusting in Him and relying on Him for grace and sustenance. Our works are always a result of our faith, not a way to earn salvation or special points with God.

According to the video, what does it mean for Jesus to be able to perfectly assess our hearts?

Why is it important not only to do good works in Jesus' name but also to do them from love for Him?

It's frightening to think we can't fool Jesus with good works. But His ability to see our sin isn't a bad thing; it's the most redemptive thing in the world. He died and rose from the dead because He already knows how sinful we are, yet He loved us so much that He died for us anyway.

If Jesus sees sin in our hearts, through the Holy Spirit He will convict us of our sins with the goal of making us more like Him. Becoming more like Jesus is always a beautiful thing, so we should welcome His conviction of our hearts. We were made to love God and others. That's Jesus' ultimate purpose in calling us to love Him first and then to do good works from that love.

If time allows, ask the group to share their thoughts on ways this study has challenged them and pointed them to Christ.

Tips for Leading a Small Group

Prayerfully Prepare

Prepare for each group session with prayer. Ask the Holy Spirit to work through you and the group discussion as you point to Jesus each week through God's Word.

REVIEW the weekly material and group questions ahead of time.

PRAY for each person in the group.

Minimize Distractions

Do everything in your ability to help people focus on what's most important: connecting with God, with the Bible, and with one another. Create a comfortable environment. If group members are uncomfortable, they'll be distracted and therefore not engaged in the group experience. Take into consideration seating, temperature, lighting, refreshments, surrounding noise, and general cleanliness.

At best, thoughtfulness and hospitality show guests and group members they're welcome and valued in whatever environment you choose to gather. At worst, people may never notice your effort, but they're also not distracted.

Include Others

Your goal is to foster a community in which people are welcome just as they are but encouraged to grow spiritually. Always be aware of opportunities to include and invite.

INCLUDE anyone who visits the group.

INVITE new people to join your group.

Encourage Discussion

A good small-group experience has the following characteristics.

EVERYONE PARTICIPATES. Encourage everyone to ask questions, share responses, or read aloud.

NO ONE DOMINATES—NOT EVEN THE LEADER. Be sure your time speaking as a leader takes up less than half your time together as a group. Politely guide discussion if anyone dominates.

NOBODY IS RUSHED THROUGH QUESTIONS. Don't feel that a moment of silence is a bad thing. People often need time to think about their responses to questions they've just heard or to gain courage to share what God is stirring in their hearts.

INPUT IS AFFIRMED AND FOLLOWED UP. Make sure you point out something true or helpful in a response. Don't just move on. Build community with follow-up questions, asking how other people have experienced similar things or how a truth has shaped their understanding of God and the Scripture you're studying. People are less likely to speak up if they fear that you don't actually want to hear their answers or that you're looking for only a certain answer.

GOD AND HIS WORD ARE CENTRAL. Opinions and experiences can be helpful, but God has given us the truth. Trust Scripture to be the authority and God's Spirit to work in people's lives. You can't change anyone, but God can. Continually point people to the Word and to active steps of faith.

KEEP CONNECTING

Think of ways to connect with group members during the week. Participation during the group session is always improved when members spend time connecting with one another outside the group sessions. The more people are comfortable with and involved in one another's lives, the more they'll look forward to being together. When people move beyond being friendly to truly being friends who form a community, they come to each session eager to engage instead of merely attending.

Encourage group members with thoughts, commitments, or questions from the session by connecting through emails, texts, and social media.

Build deeper friendships by planning or spontaneously inviting group members to join you outside your regularly scheduled group time for meals; fun activities; and projects around your home, church, or community.

Group Information

NAME   **CONTACT**

DISCIPLE FOR LIFE

The Disciple for Life series emphasizes modeling and practice without compromising biblical knowledge or redemptive community. Each study includes short videos, a leader guide that identifies core principles and elements of effective small-group leadership, and content for growing as a disciple for life.

BASICS

Understanding the Foundations of a Healthy Church
6 sessions

Get a comprehensive understanding of the church and its organization and practices.

Bible Study Book 006104044 $12.99
Leader Kit 006104045 $39.99

KNOWING JESUS

Living by His Name
6 sessions

Move toward a more intimate relationship with Jesus through His miracles, what He said about Himself, and what others said about Him.

Bible Study Book 005791554 $12.99
Leader Kit 005791555 $39.99

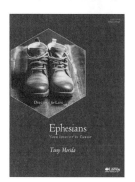

EPHESIANS

Your Identity in Christ
6 sessions

Get practical answers to contemporary believers' basic questions about the Christian life.

Bible Study Book 005792212 $12.99
Leader Kit 005792213 $39.99